GREAT EXPLORERS

Written by **STEWART ROSS** • Illustrated by **STEPHEN BIESTY**

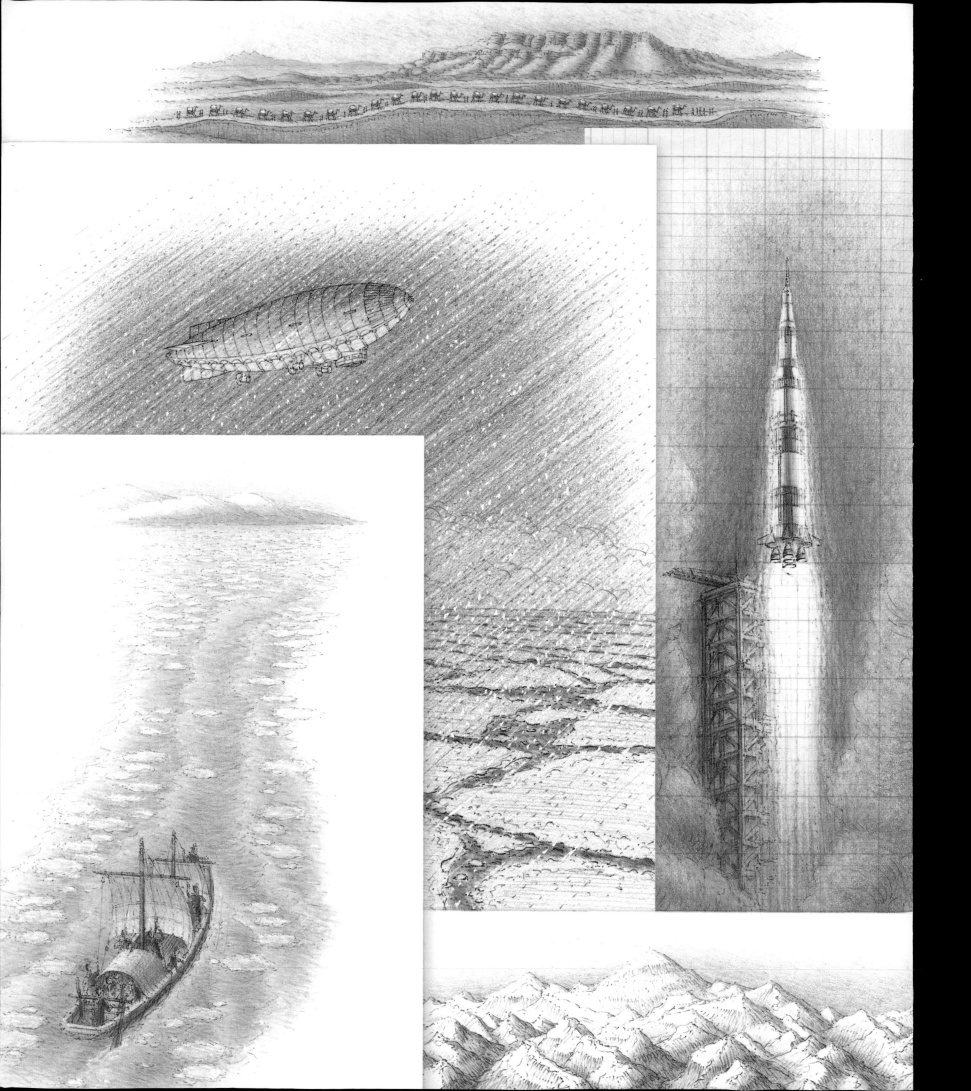

CONTENTS

INTRODUCTION

For most of human history, people knew almost nothing about the planet they inhabited. They did not even know what a planet was.

All they understood was the area around where they lived: the woods, fields, hills, rivers and perhaps a stretch of shore that gave on to a blank ocean.

Around 5,000 years ago, our ancestors started to explore, and very slowly their understanding grew. Step by step, they built up a picture of the world, like assembling a gigantic jigsaw puzzle or watching graphics download on to a computer screen.

Of all the many journeys of exploration that revealed the world to us, this book concentrates on just a handful. They are not necessarily the most important in terms of what they found, but each one is extraordinary for the way that it was made.

We start with Pytheas the Greek, who probably reached the Arctic in a boat so simple it was little more than a tub. He was one of the earliest explorers to make a record of where he went and how he travelled.

Next comes the story of a Viking, Leif Eriksson. The Vikings were the first Europeans to reach America and perhaps the most skilful sailors ever to sail the seas.

Our first overland explorer is Marco Polo, an Italian merchant who crossed the deserts of Asia with caravans of camels. He left an account that inspired generations of future explorers.

The magnificent junks commanded by the

Chinese Admiral Zheng He were equipped with stern-post rudders and magnetic compasses, advances that changed ships for ever. The Portuguese caravels and carracks that carried Christopher Columbus to the Caribbean and Ferdinand Magellan's brave crew all the way round the world could not have done so without them.

By sailing right round it, Magellan's expedition proved once and for all that the earth is a sphere. From then on, exploration changed. It began to be as much about information-gathering as about discovering new lands. James Cook did not discover New Zealand or the north-east coast of Australia, but by carefully charting their coasts he transformed people's understanding of them.

David Livingstone, another great geographer, did the same in central Africa. He and a later explorer, Mary Kingsley, travelled to the interior of this vast continent by steamboat, a technology specially suited for river exploration.

Technology advanced rapidly in the twentieth century, and with it exploration. Engine-powered flight took Umberto Nobile over the icy wastes of the North Pole. The invention of a pressurized cabin allowed Auguste Piccard to soar to the stratosphere in a gas-filled balloon, and his son Jacques to plunge to the ocean floor in a bathyscaphe. The technology of oxygen supply used by the Piccards also helped Edmund Hillary and Tenzing Norgay scale the highest point on the earth's surface, Mount Everest.

Finally, in 1969, the crew of NASA's Apollo 11 mission succeeded in perhaps the most daring adventure of all: using rocket power, they landed on the moon and returned safely to Earth.

As well as technological advance, the story of exploration is about people. The courage and determination of the individual men and women in this book are why we know so much about the beauty, majesty and mystery of our world.

TO THE FROZEN NORTH

Pytheas the Greek sails to Ultima Thule, around 340 BC

We begin over 2,000 years ago.

In a city on the edge of the Mediterranean Sea, there lived a Greek explorer named Pytheas. Almost nothing is known of him. Historians cannot say precisely when he lived, what he looked like, whether he was rich or poor, and they don't even know exactly where he went. All they can say for certain is that he made a remarkable voyage north to a place where he thought the sea looked like curdled milk, and that when he returned home, he wrote about it in a book called *On the Ocean*.

Sadly, all copies of Pytheas' account have disappeared. It obviously caused a stir in the classical world, though, because in works that *do* survive, at least 18 other writers mention it. One of them, the Greek geographer Strabo, described Pytheas as a fraud and *"the worst possible liar"*. Others believed he was telling the truth – and today most historians agree, which is why he is often called the first great explorer.

Using every mention of *On the Ocean* by those who read it in ancient times, modern scholars have tried to piece together where Pytheas went and why. His home town was Massalia, the southern French port we now call Marseilles. Like many people there, he was almost certainly a merchant, which means he probably traded in two precious imports: amber and tin. The Greeks used yellow-gold amber to fashion jewellery and ornaments, and they melted down bars of gleaming tin and mixed it with small quantities of copper to make bronze.

Since amber and tin came from lands north of the Mediterranean, it seems likely that Pytheas began his journey for reasons of trade. Historians know that he travelled first to south-west Britain, a place where tin was mined. They have no idea how he got there, though. He may have taken a ship of his own, a Mediterranean trading vessel, through the Straits of Gibraltar (which the Greeks called the Pillars of Hercules) to the west coast of Spain. Or he might have sailed on a swift Greek warship to the mouth of the River Aude, then crossed France by riverboat.

Both journeys would have brought him to the Atlantic coast, where he probably picked up a more sturdy Celtic craft to take him to southern Britain. To ride out Atlantic storms, these were tough vessels with hefty main timbers 305 millimetres thick. Their strong oak planks and shallow draught allowed them to rest on the bottom of the sea when tides ran low.

From the tin mines of

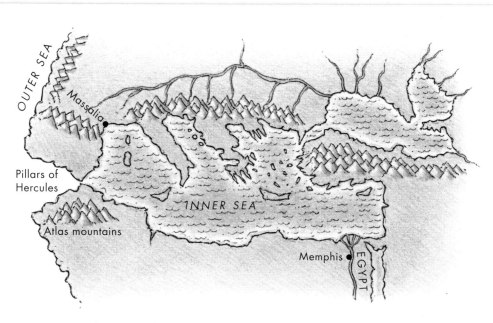

This map of the ancient Greek world shows their Inner Sea (our Mediterranean Sea and Black Sea) and the Pillars of Hercules (the Straits of Gibraltar), beyond which lay an Outer Sea and the unknown…

Cornwall, Pytheas continued north up the west coast of the British Isles. Almost certainly he made this part of his journey in a local boat called a currach. This craft looked like a sort of giant basket: its hull was woven wickerwork covered with buttered ox hides, sewn together and made waterproof at the joints with pitch. Driven by leather sails or rows of oars, a currach was light enough to skip over towering waves like a sea bird. Ships of this design were still in use in the twentieth century and were said to ride out storms that sank the toughest lifeboats. All that bobbing would have had one major disadvantage, though: Pytheas would probably have been horribly seasick.

Further and further Pytheas sailed, through mists and icy gales – up the Irish Sea, past the Isle of Man and on to the Western Isles of Scotland. He would have had no map to guide him, but travelling in a northerly direction was not difficult: by day, he had simply to keep the sun at his back, and by night, to follow the North Star. Historians know that he didn't just stare at the wild and rocky coast from his vessel, either, but went ashore for weeks on end, writing about the people he met, keeping a record of where he travelled and estimating distances to work out how far he had come.

For as well as being a merchant and explorer, Pytheas was a skilled geographer. The Greeks knew that the world was round, and realized that the length of a shadow increases as you go north. To work out how much further north than Massalia he was, Pytheas used a wooden staff of fixed length, called a gnomon. He remembered the length of its midday shadow at certain times of the year back home. So, at regular intervals during his journey, he placed his gnomon upright on level ground at noon and measured how long its shadow was.

As some of Pytheas' calculations have survived in the writings of others, it should be possible to work out where he took his gnomon readings. Unfortunately, he recorded his position in "stades", units of measurement that varied from place to place. Scholars believe he

SOME OF THE SHIPS PYTHEAS MAY HAVE USED TO TRAVEL TO BRITAIN AND BEYOND

A trading vessel of the type used by merchants all over the Mediterranean. It was steered by large paddles at the stern.

A Greek warship powered by a sail and rows of oars. The bronze ram at the bow was for attacking enemy vessels.

A cargo-carrying riverboat used for trading on the many large rivers flowing into the Mediterranean.

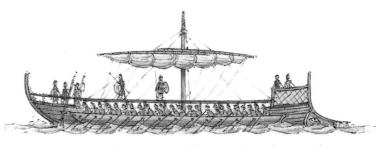

A powerfully-built Celtic vessel: its tough construction enabled it to survive in the stormy waters of the Atlantic.

A local skin-covered currach or coracle used by the Celts of Ireland and northern Britain.

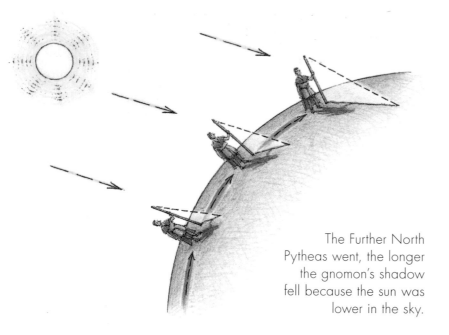

The Further North Pytheas went, the longer the gnomon's shadow fell because the sun was lower in the sky.

probably made his most northerly gnomon measurement at the furthest tip of Scotland.

Where did he go after that? In *On the Ocean*, Pytheas wrote that he reached Ultima Thule – *"the most remote of places"*. No one has been able to work out for certain where this was. Pliny the Elder, a Roman writer who had read *On the Ocean*, thought it was *"at the top of the world ... six days' voyage to the north of Britain"*. Some historians think Thule was the Orkney Islands. Others have suggested Norway. The most likely answer seems to be that Pytheas travelled northwest across the stormy Atlantic as far as Iceland.

From there, Pytheas may have sailed still further north, into the Arctic. According to the Ancient Greek writer Polybius, Pytheas said that where he went *"the earth did not exist on its own, nor sea nor mist, but instead all were mixed together like a marine lung"*. Wherever this was, the image of the semi-frozen sea breathing like a lung is one of the most powerful in the whole history of exploration. And for Pytheas to have travelled so far from home and his own civilization was little short of amazing. ✹

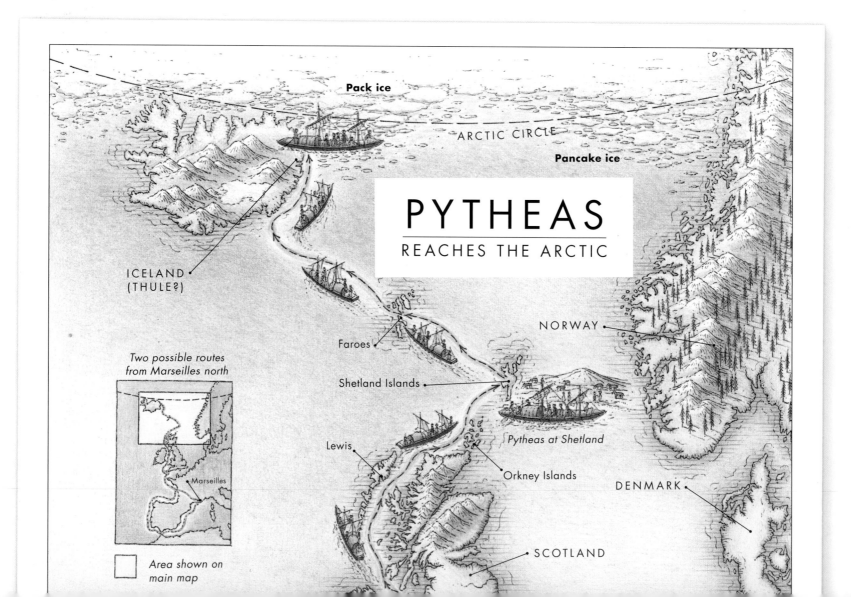

Pack ice

ARCTIC CIRCLE

Pancake ice

PYTHEAS
REACHES THE ARCTIC

ICELAND (THULE?)

NORWAY

Two possible routes from Marseilles north

Faroes

Shetland Islands

Pytheas at Shetland

Lewis

Orkney Islands

DENMARK

Marseilles

SCOTLAND

☐ Area shown on main map

BUILDING A CURRACH

Most boats were built from the bottom up, but currach builders worked the other way round.
They started with the gunwale (the rim of the hull) and built the body of the boat upside down.

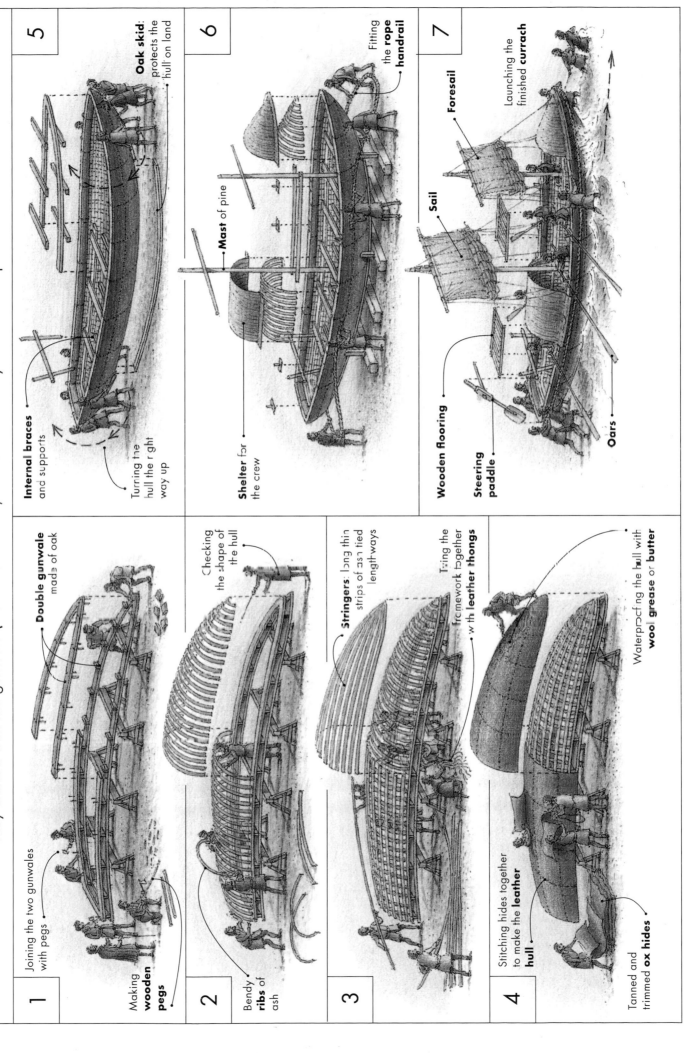

1

Joining the two gunwales with pegs

Making **wooden pegs**

Double gunwale made of oak

2

Bendy **ribs** of ash

Checking the shape of the hull

3

Stringers: long thin strips of ash tied lengthways

Tying the framework together with **leather thongs**

4

Stitching hides together to make the leather **hull**

Tanned and trimmed **ox hides**

Waterproofing the hull with **wool grease** or **butter**

5

Turning the hull the right way up

Internal braces and supports

Oak skid: protects the hull on land

6

Shelter for the crew

Mast of pine

Fitting the **rope handrail**

7

Launching the finished **currach**

Foresail

Sail

Wooden flooring

Steering paddle

Oars

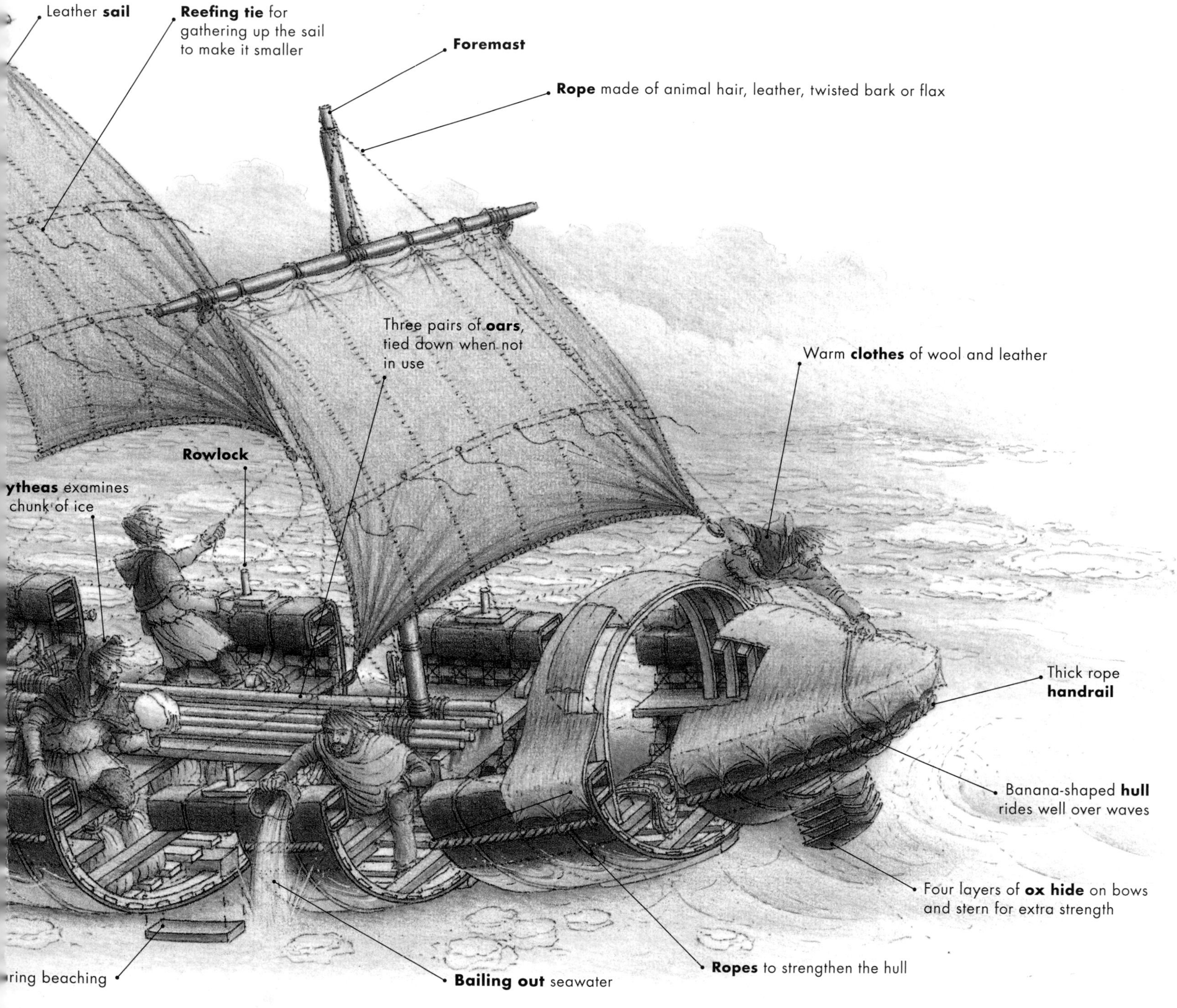

Leather **sail**

Reefing tie for gathering up the sail to make it smaller

Foremast

Rope made of animal hair, leather, twisted bark or flax

Three pairs of **oars**, tied down when not in use

Warm **clothes** of wool and leather

Rowlock

ytheas examines chunk of ice

Thick rope **handrail**

Banana-shaped **hull** rides well over waves

Four layers of **ox hide** on bows and stern for extra strength

ring beaching

Bailing out seawater

Ropes to strengthen the hull

Dried fish

Fruit

Ox hides for repairs

Wool grease or butter for waterproofing hides

A CURRACH IN AN ICY SEA

Travelling into the Arctic, where the sea is dotted with sharp pieces of pancake ice, Pytheas' fragile craft needed to proceed with great caution.

Mainmast

Shelter for crew and passengers

Captain steering the boat with a tiller stick

Steering paddle

Ox hide wrapped over **double gunwale**

Crew eating porridge

Hides stitched together with cord made from flax

Stringers

Ash ribs lashed together with leather thongs

Stores

Oak skid: protects the hull d

STORES FOR THE JOURNEY

Supplies that Pytheas and his crew took with them included a change of clothing, materials for repairing the ship, and food. Perishable food was preserved by drying, smoking, salting, pickling or baking and stored in sacks or earthenware pots.

Sack of spare clothes

Leather water bottle

Bread

Oats

THE MYSTERY OF VINLAND

Leif Eriksson reaches the coast of America, AD 1003

Over a thousand years after Pytheas sailed into the Arctic Ocean, local bands of warrior Vikings, or "Norsemen", set out in the opposite direction. In search of fertile land and a better life, they sailed south from their homelands in Scandinavia and forcibly occupied large areas of Britain, Ireland and France.

In the ninth century, other Vikings explored westward, reaching Iceland. From there a Norse captain, Erik the Red, sailed on to Greenland and established the first settlement there, around AD 982. (The land was actually bleak and barren, but he called it "green" to entice others to follow him.)

The North Atlantic, with its cold waters, mountainous waves and floating ice, is one of the most hazardous waterways in the world. So how, all those centuries ago, did Viking mariners sail hundreds, even thousands of kilometres across its uncharted vastness? The answer is that they were both superb seamen and brilliant boatbuilders.

The ships that brought Erik the Red and other settlers to Greenland were not the famous Viking longships with dragon heads carved on their prows, striped sails and rows of shields along their sides. Instead,

The knarr's construction meant it could move with the sea. The skin of the hull, made up of overlapping strakes, was tied rather than nailed to the ribs and beams beneath it. These looser fixings gave the hull flexibility.

they sailed in shorter trading vessels, known as knarrs. A knarr was deeper than a longship and could carry around 30 people, as well as equipment, cattle, food and water, and everything necessary to make repairs. (Give a Viking a suitable tree and some carpentry tools, and in two shakes he could knock up any part of a boat you wanted.)

The most remarkable thing about the knarr was that it was designed to move with the power of the sea, rather than challenge it. The only rigid part of the boat was its oak keel. On either side, some 16 overlapping planks were riveted together to make a flexible hull that could accept the shocks and buffets of the waves by twisting like a fish.

Some 20 years after Erik the Red had established his settlement in Greenland, a man named Bjarni Herjolfsson sailed from Iceland to visit his family. The Norse sea gods did not give him and his crew an easy time. Their knarr was first buffeted by gales, then lost in fog until, as the *Saga of Erik the Red* recalls, *"they knew not whither they were drifting"*. When they eventually reached Greenland, Bjarni had a strange tale to tell. Somewhere to the west, he reported, was the wooded coastline of a land previously unknown to the Vikings.

One who heard Bjarni's story was Erik the Red's son, Leif (also called Leif the Lucky). Eager for adventure, he bought Bjarni's knarr from him, gathered a crew and set out to explore the mysterious new coast.

But without maps or compasses, how did he know where to steer his ship? Within sight of the shore, direction-finding was easy. The difficulty started when there were no landmarks left to steer by. By day, the Vikings could gather information from the sun, which they knew rose in the east, set in the west and at noon stood due south. By night there was the Pole Star, which always lay due north. Experienced sailors used

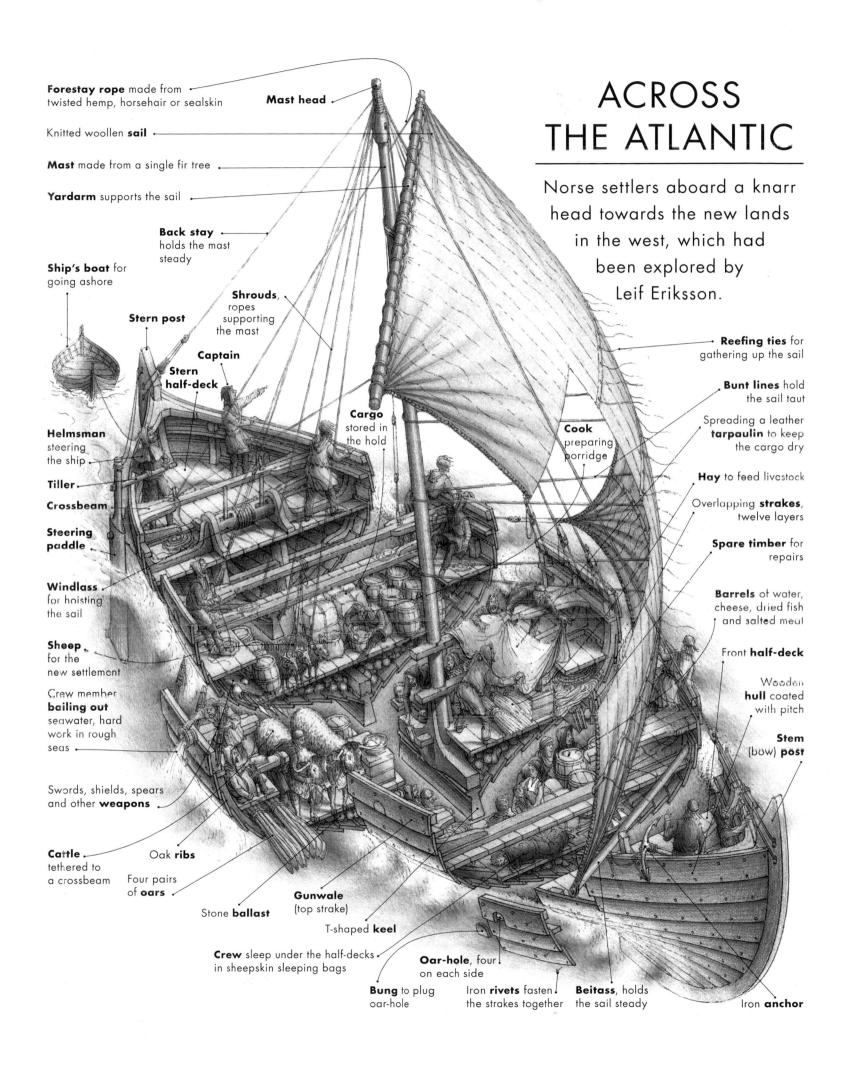

Forestay rope made from twisted hemp, horsehair or sealskin

Mast head

Knitted woollen sail

Mast made from a single fir tree

Yardarm supports the sail

Back stay holds the mast steady

Ship's boat for going ashore

Shrouds, ropes supporting the mast

Stern post

Captain

Stern half-deck

Helmsman steering the ship

Tiller

Crossbeam

Steering paddle

Windlass for hoisting the sail

Sheep for the new settlement

Crew member bailing out seawater, hard work in rough seas

Swords, shields, spears and other weapons

Cattle tethered to a crossbeam

Oak ribs

Four pairs of oars

Stone ballast

Gunwale (top strake)

T-shaped keel

Crew sleep under the half-decks in sheepskin sleeping bags

Bung to plug oar-hole

Oar-hole, four on each side

Iron rivets fasten the strakes together

Beitass, holds the sail steady

Cargo stored in the hold

Cook preparing porridge

ACROSS THE ATLANTIC

Norse settlers aboard a knarr head towards the new lands in the west, which had been explored by Leif Eriksson.

Reefing ties for gathering up the sail

Bunt lines hold the sail taut

Spreading a leather tarpaulin to keep the cargo dry

Hay to feed livestock

Overlapping strakes, twelve layers

Spare timber for repairs

Barrels of water, cheese, dried fish and salted meat

Front half-deck

Wooden hull coated with pitch

Stem (bow) post

Iron anchor

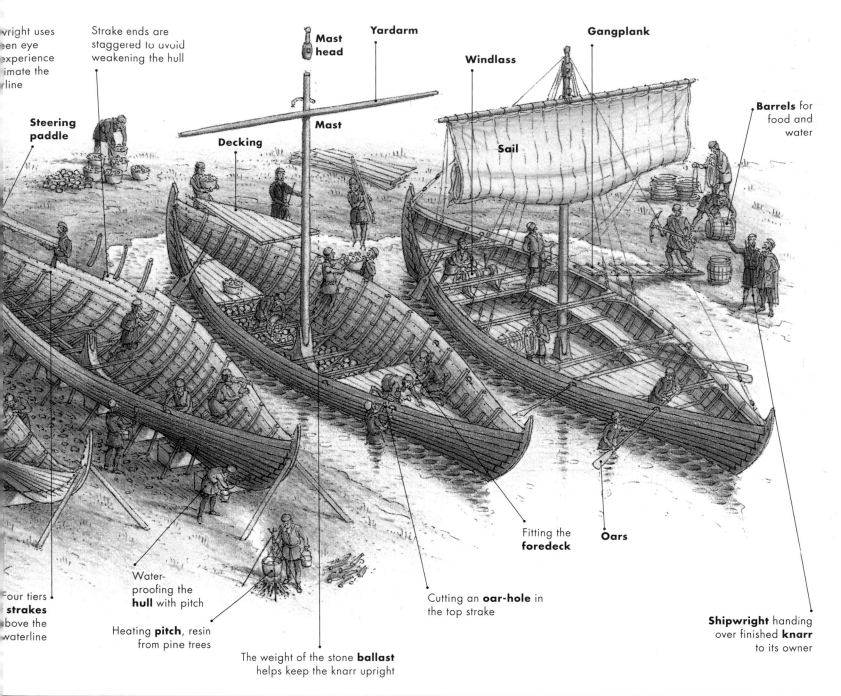

...wright uses ...een eye ...experience ...imate the ...rline

Steering paddle

Strake ends are staggered to avoid weakening the hull

Mast head

Yardarm

Mast

Decking

Gangplank

Windlass

Sail

Barrels for food and water

Four tiers ...strakes ...bove the ...waterline

Water-proofing the **hull** with pitch

Heating **pitch**, resin from pine trees

The weight of the stone **ballast** helps keep the knarr upright

Cutting an **oar-hole** in the top strake

Fitting the **foredeck**

Oars

Shipwright handing over finished **knarr** to its owner

T'S TOOLS

...a saw, but split it along the grain.

...he shipwright used a moulding ...n to make grooves for caulking.

He made pilot holes for nails or rivets with an auger.

The strakes were nailed together with a hammer ...

and waterproofed with pine tar.

SHIP-BUILDING, VIKING STYLE

With a flexible hull built around its sturdy oak keel, the knarr was the most seaworthy craft of its generation.

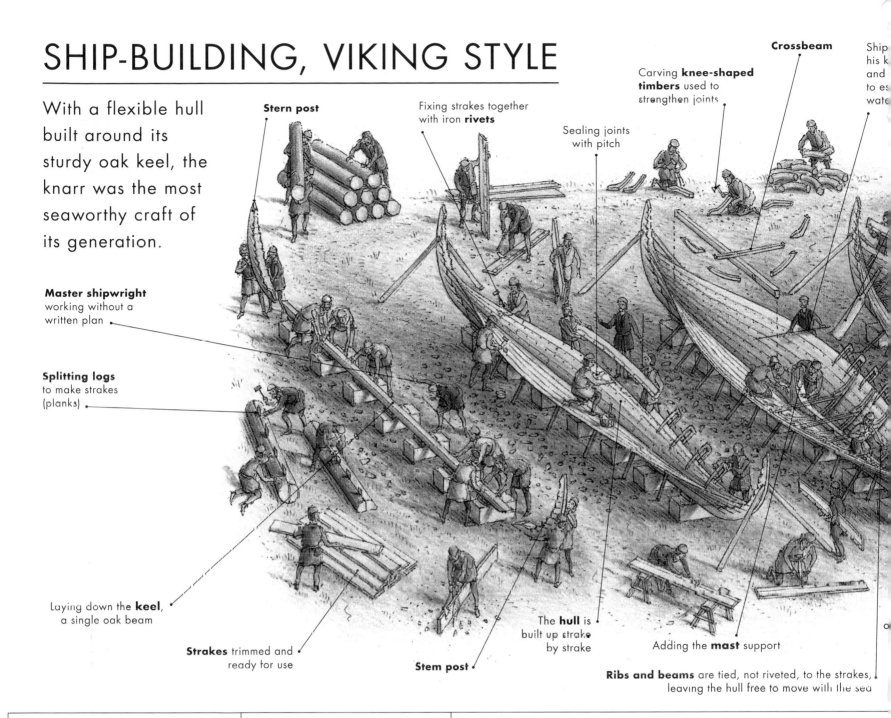

Stern post

Fixing strakes together with iron **rivets**

Sealing joints with pitch

Carving **knee-shaped timbers** used to strengthen joints

Crossbeam

Shi... his k and... to e... wate...

Master shipwright working without a written plan

Splitting logs to make strakes (planks)

Laying down the **keel**, a single oak beam

Strakes trimmed and ready for use

Stem post

The **hull** is built up strake by strake

Adding the **mast** support

Ribs and beams are tied, not riveted, to the strakes, leaving the hull free to move with the sea

---

A plank, or strake, was split from a log using a mallet and wedges ...

then thinned with a side-axe ...

shaped with an adze ...

A SHIPWRIGH...
Viking shipwrights never cut wood with...

and smoothed with a draw-knife.

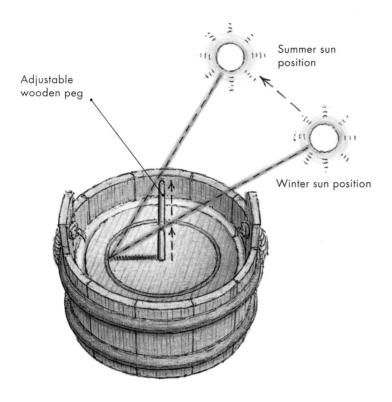

Adjustable wooden peg

Summer sun position

Winter sun position

The only navigational tool the Vikings may have used to help them cross the ocean was a sun-shadow board. In the middle of the wooden dial was a peg which they would raise in summer and lower in winter. At noon, they would put the instrument in a bucket of water (so it stayed level), and watch the shadow cast across the peg by the sun. A circle on the board marked where the shadow should reach if the ship was sailing at the right latitude. If the shadow crossed the circle, then the ship was too far north; if it stayed inside the circle, it was too far south.

other knowledge, too. They learnt a good deal from the direction and temperature of the wind (a cold wind generally came from the north), the colour of the sea, the shapes of the waves, the kinds of birds and fish they saw and whether or not there was ice in the water.

But when a violent storm blew up, the sun and stars were blacked out, the sea became a roaring monster and visibility was no more than a few metres. This was a seaman's nightmare, and the Vikings had a special word for it: "hafvilla", meaning not having a clue where you were going. When that happened, the crew cried out to their gods, bailed frantically to keep their ship

afloat and eked out their supplies of water, butter, bread and oatmeal porridge as best they could. If the storm blew out in good time, there was a chance they might make landfall; if it did not, they were never seen again.

Fortunately for Leif, the sagas that tell his story record that the weather stayed fair, and that after a smooth crossing he reached what was probably Baffin Island, off the coast of Canada. He named it Helluland or "Slabland" because of the flat stones he saw there. Sailing down the coast of Labrador, he reached a wooded shore and is reported to have said, *"This land shall have a name after its nature; and we will call it Markland"* (meaning "Forestland"). Exploring still further south, he came to a mild and verdant region (possibly somewhere in New England) which he called "Vinland" after the vines or berries growing there.

Leif and his crew spent the winter in Vinland, before returning home with news of what they had found. Larger expeditions followed and established settlements. But it seems that none of them lasted long, and by the eleventh century, Viking exploration of the new land had been abandoned.

Although Leif reached the Americas 500 years before Christopher Columbus, for centuries people believed that Columbus had "discovered America". The reason for the misunderstanding is that the stories of the Viking voyages were recorded only in spoken sagas – long poems passed down from generation to generation. When these were eventually written down, it was in the Old Icelandic language that few outside Scandinavia and Iceland understood.

Scholars first began translating and studying the sagas in the twentieth century and when they came across Leif's extraordinary story, they didn't know what to make of it. In 1957, the mystery deepened with the discovery of a strange map of the world. It appeared to be very old and marked on it, to the west of Greenland, was a place labelled "Vinland". Experts were divided. Some said the so-called Vinland Map was genuine and

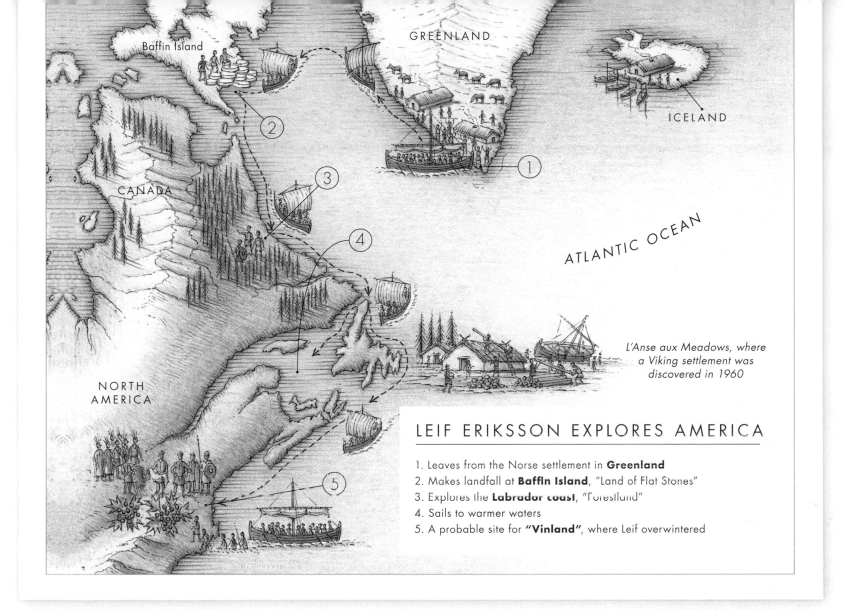

GREENLAND

Baffin Island

ICELAND

CANADA

②

③

④

ATLANTIC OCEAN

NORTH
AMERICA

⑤

*L'Anse aux Meadows, where
a Viking settlement was
discovered in 1960*

LEIF ERIKSSON EXPLORES AMERICA

1. Leaves from the Norse settlement in **Greenland**
2. Makes landfall at **Baffin Island**, "Land of Flat Stones"
3. Explores the **Labrador coast**, "Forestland"
4. Sails to warmer waters
5. A probable site for **"Vinland"**, where Leif overwintered

backed up the claims made in the *Saga of Erik the Red*; others pronounced it a forgery.

In the end, whether the map was genuine or not did not matter. During the 1960s, Norwegian archaeologists uncovered the remains of a Viking settlement at L'Anse aux Meadows in Newfoundland, Canada. This remarkable discovery finally proved that the sagas had been right all along – Leif Eriksson and the Vikings really had been the first European explorers to set foot in America. ⊕

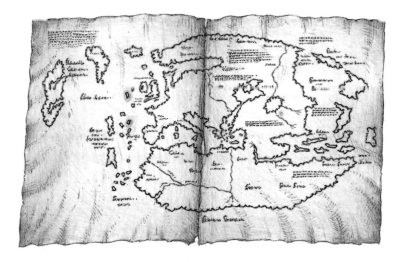

In 1957, the "Vinland Map" was sold by an antiquarian bookseller to Paul Mellon, an American millionaire. The bookseller claimed it was a fifteenth-century copy of a thirteenth-century map of the world.

RIDING THE SILK ROAD

Marco Polo's adventures in Asia, 1271–74

Exploring is not necessarily about finding places that you never knew existed. Think of the moon, for example. Human beings have always known it was there, but astronauts didn't explore it until 1969. For medieval Europeans, much of Asia and the Far East might as well have been the moon. They had heard of countries called Persia and China, but knew next to nothing about them.

So it is surprising to discover that China and Europe had been trading since Roman times. The key to it all was silk. This beautiful material is woven from thread taken from the cocoon of a moth that feeds on the leaves of the mulberry tree. Chinese silk was finer than all others, and the Chinese guarded the secrets of its manufacture closely.

Wealthy Europeans had always loved to dress or sleep in silk, and every year bales of it were transported overland and sold for huge sums. Back in the other direction – west to east – went goods such as horses, wool, silver and gold. Over the centuries, a network of tracks came to criss-cross the vast expanse of Asia. Together, they came to be known as the Silk Road.

While the goods travelled thousands of kilometres, few of the merchants did. Instead, a trader would buy something of value, transport it part of the way, then sell it on to another trader who would do the same. (As each merchant made a profit, the further an item went the more expensive it became.) This was partly for convenience – the distance between the Chinese capital,

Peking (Beijing), and the great trading port of Venice was around 8,500 kilometres – and partly for safety: the routes could be extremely dangerous. Highwaymen and bandits preyed on the traders, ambushing and sometimes killing them to rob them of their goods.

In the twelfth century, however, a fierce Mongol leader, Genghis Khan (*c.* 1162–1227), conquered a vast area of central Asia, including most of the territory through which the Silk Road passed. The emperor's officers cracked down on lawlessness, and the routes grew safer – tempting adventurers of all kinds out onto the road to seek their fortunes.

Among them were two merchants from Venice. Between 1250 and 1269, Niccolo and Maffeo Polo travelled widely in Asia and even reached the court of Genghis' grandson, Kublai Khan, emperor of all China. Curious about the west, the "Great Khan", as he was also known, sent the brothers back to Italy as his ambassadors, requesting that they return with messages from their pope and oil from the lamp at the Holy Sepulchre in Jerusalem. The Polos agreed.

In 1271 the Polo brothers set out on their second journey to China. This time they took with them Niccolo's 17-year-old son, Marco. Many years later, an account of Marco's journeys, *Il Milione* (usually translated as *The Travels of Marco Polo)*, would become one of the most popular books in Europe and is still in print today.

It is almost impossible for us to imagine what an exhausting and dangerous journey Marco had undertaken. *Il Milione* tells us very little about how the party actually travelled. But *The Practice of Marketing*, a handbook written by a contemporary of Marco Polo's, is full of useful advice: the author recommended taking at least two servants on the journey, ample provisions of water, flour and salt fish, and money in the form of gold or silver coins. He also advised hiring local guide-interpreters called "dragomans" along the way, and following local custom in matters of dress and beard style.

Only the very poor or foolish travelled the paths of the Silk Road on foot. If walkers were not mugged by thieves, they stood a good chance of freezing to death in the highlands, dying of thirst in the deserts or simply dropping dead from exhaustion. So where the tracks were in good condition and there was plenty of food and water, the Polos rode on horseback. In the mountains, they swapped their horses for hardy little donkeys. Across deserts, they relied on camels, either riding or sitting in carts pulled behind them. A camel can go for a week without water, and its broad feet can tread even the finest sand without sinking in.

Most of the time, for safety and company, the Polos travelled with others – as part of a "caravan". This was a group of merchants escorting a long train of pack animals – sometimes as many as 400 – roped together in a long line. Plodding along at a steady pace, a caravan might cover 30 kilometres a day. At night, it entered into the courtyard of a fortified resting-place called a caravanserai. Here the animals rested and were fed, while servants locked away the precious merchandise in secure storerooms.

Il Milione contained no maps either, so it is hard to be sure of the Polos' exact route. But they certainly went to Jerusalem, to collect the holy oil that Kublai Khan had asked for, before turning north into the rugged mountains that lie between the Black and Caspian seas. From there they seem to have swung south again, skirting the deserts of Arabia and cutting down

Beasts of burden: The sturdy donkey and the swifter horse were the favoured pack animals outside desert areas.

through Mesopotamia (Iraq) and Persia (Iran) to the city of Hormuz, whose port, Marco said, *"is frequented by traders from all parts of India who bring … precious stones, pearls, gold tissues, elephants' teeth and various other articles of merchandise"*.

From Hormuz they headed north again to pick up the main tracks going east. They made slow progress, sometimes stopping in a town or village for months. Some scholars believe they may have stayed in Afghanistan for as long as a year because Marco had caught malaria and was too ill to travel. Next, they proceeded to Kashmir and then to the high Pamir Mountains, where Marco noticed that *"fires when lighted do not give the same heat as in lower situations, nor produce the same effect in cooking food"*. He thought this was an effect of the cold. In fact it was an effect of altitude – as climbers on Mount Everest were to discover again centuries later.

A camel cart brings fodder for the pack animals of a caravan.

A CARAVAN ON THE MOVE

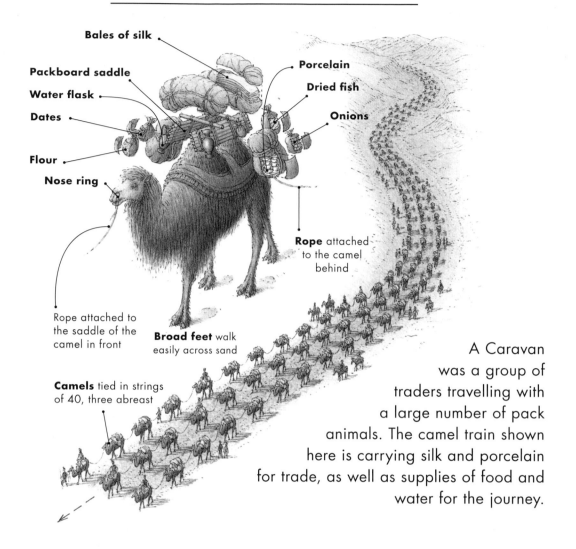

Bales of silk

Packboard saddle

Water flask

Dates

Flour

Nose ring

Porcelain

Dried fish

Onions

Rope attached to the camel behind

Rope attached to the saddle of the camel in front

Broad feet walk easily across sand

Camels tied in strings of 40, three abreast

A Caravan was a group of traders travelling with a large number of pack animals. The camel train shown here is carrying silk and porcelain for trade, as well as supplies of food and water for the journey.

travelled holy oil from Jerusalem. The emperor, perhaps impressed that these hardy men had managed to make the long journey east not once but twice, invited them to stay and travel freely within his empire. This they did for many years.

Finally, around 1292, the Polos set out for home again. This time they went mainly by sea – following alternative trade routes for goods moving between Asia and Europe – and reached Venice three years later. By now, Marco was a middle-aged man and his friends and family did not recognize him. They found it hard to believe the stories he had to tell, too.

A few years later, Marco was captured by rival merchants in a sea battle and imprisoned in the port of Genoa. There he told the writer Rustichello, a fellow prisoner, about his journeys in the East. Rustichello wrote down what he heard.

The toughest part of the Polos' expedition was across the bleak and barren land just west of the Chinese frontier. In the terrible Takla Makan and Gobi deserts they sometimes went for days without finding an oasis at which to fill their water bottles. When the oases dried up completely, as happened from time to time, desperate travellers would drink the milk and even the blood of their animals. Beside the track lay the bleached skeletons of men and beasts who had not made it.

The Polos *did* make it. They entered China near the Great Wall and proceeded to Shangdu, Kublai Khan's summer residence. Here, with much ceremony, they handed over letters from the Pope and the much-

Although Marco Polo always said he had not told Rustichello even half of what he'd seen for fear of being thought a liar, *Il Milione* was an instant success. It changed the way Europeans thought about the world and inspired later generations to undertake explorations of their own. Its influence was particularly strong on a certain Italian sailor who dreamed of finding a new way to China and the East. The dreamer's name was Christopher Columbus. ✪

INSIDE A CARAVANSERAI

This secure place of refuge bustles with activity as a caravan, like one the Polos travelled with, arrives and prepares to settle down for the night. The word caravanserai comes from the Persian "karwan" (caravan) and "sarai" meaning an inn.

A scale drawing of a caravanserai

The silk routes were dotted with caravanserais. There was one every 30 kilometres or so – which was around a day's journey for a caravan. It provided a lodging place for people and beasts, and overnight storage for valuable trade goods.

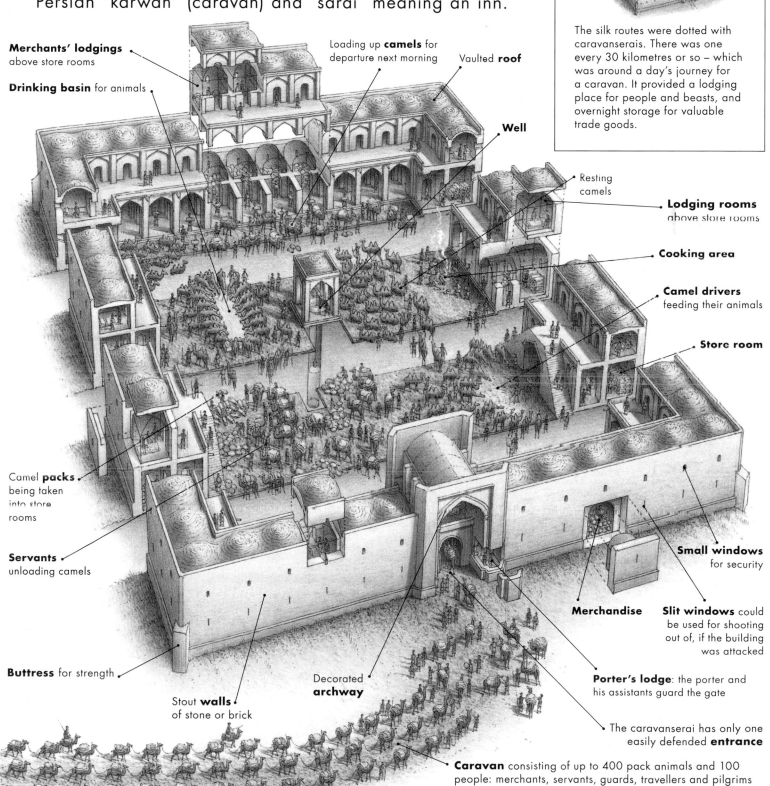

Merchants' lodgings above store rooms

Drinking basin for animals

Loading up **camels** for departure next morning

Vaulted **roof**

Well

Resting camels

Lodging rooms above store rooms

Cooking area

Camel drivers feeding their animals

Store room

Camel **packs** being taken into store rooms

Servants unloading camels

Buttress for strength

Stout **walls** of stone or brick

Decorated **archway**

Merchandise

Small windows for security

Slit windows could be used for shooting out of, if the building was attacked

Porter's lodge: the porter and his assistants guard the gate

The caravanserai has only one easily defended **entrance**

Caravan consisting of up to 400 pack animals and 100 people: merchants, servants, guards, travellers and pilgrims

SILK ROAD TO CHINA

fway across the world. On the way out, he followed
s mountains to the court of the great Kublai Khan.

co falls ill in the **mountains**, where he notices that fire burns less well
ing the deadly **Takla Makan Desert**
ugh the **Great Wall of China**
arrive at Kublai Khan's summer palace at **Shangdu**

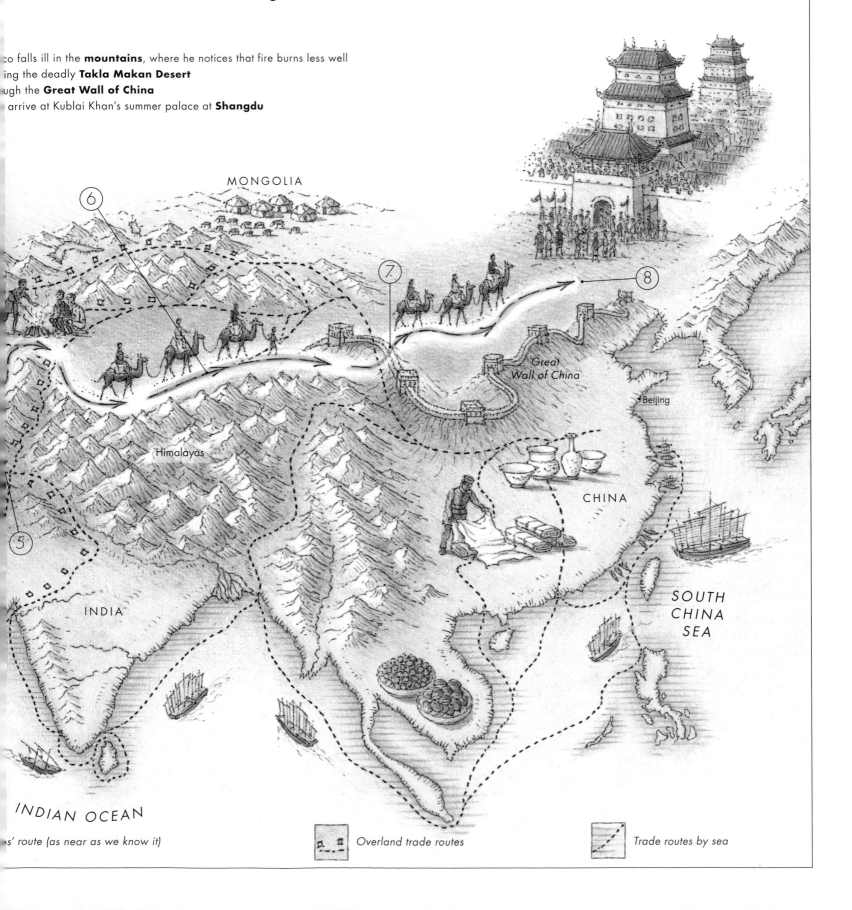

MONGOLIA

CHINA

Great
Wall of China

Beijing

Himalayas

INDIA

SOUTH
CHINA
SEA

INDIAN OCEAN

s' route (as near as we know it)

Overland trade routes

Trade routes by sea

Marco Polo's incredible 8,000-kilometre journey took him hal
the network of tracks that snaked through deserts and acro

1. Marco, his father and his uncle set sail from **Venice**
2. They receive letters for the Khan from Pope Gregory X at **Acre**
3. They collect holy oil in **Jerusalem**
4. Leaving **Hormuz**, the Polos join a caravan travelling north

5. Mar
6. Bra
7. Thro
8. The

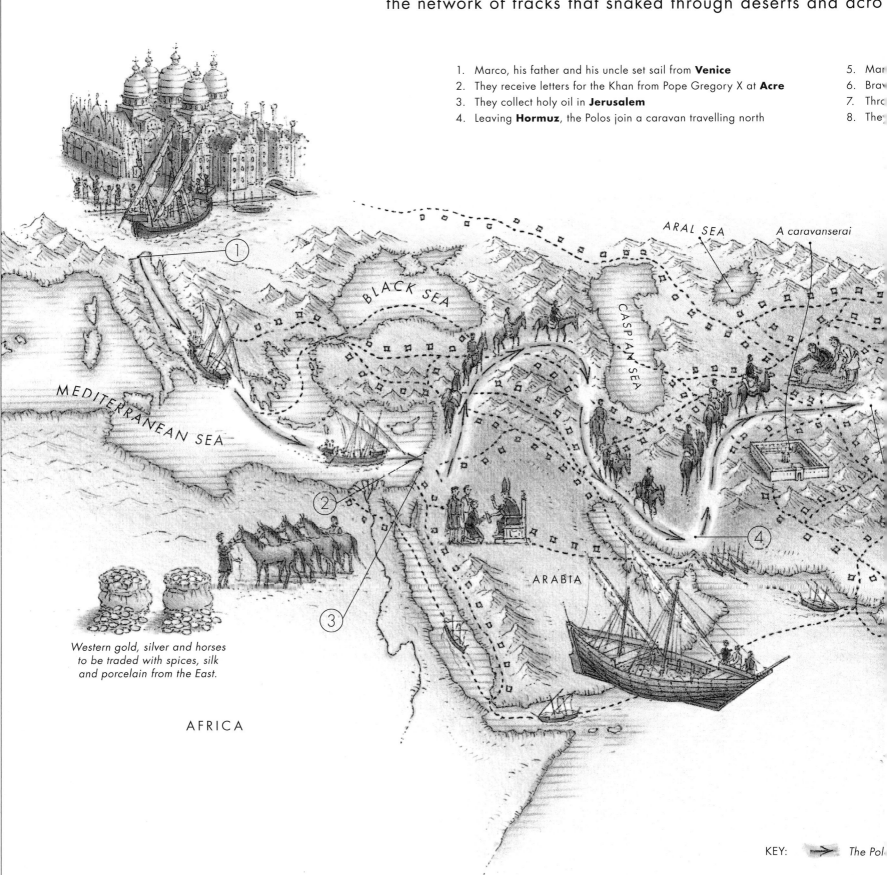

ARAL SEA

A caravanserai

BLACK SEA

CASPIAN SEA

MEDITERRANEAN SEA

ARABIA

*Western gold, silver and horses
to be traded with spices, silk
and porcelain from the East.*

AFRICA

KEY: → *The Pol*

FROM CHINA TO INDIA

Zheng He's Treasure Fleet crosses the Western Sea, 1405–07

Kublai Khan, the great emperor of China whom Marco Polo had admired so much, died in 1294. Seventy years later the Mongol dynasty he had founded collapsed. It was replaced by a native Chinese dynasty, the Ming (meaning "shining bright") dynasty.

The Great Khan had believed in sea power as a way to defend China, spread its power abroad and help foreign trade. His soldiers and merchants sailed the Indian Ocean (which they called the Western Sea) in gigantic ships known as junks. These vessels each had four masts and nine sails, and carried a crew of over 200 men.

In 1402, Zhu Di, the third Ming ruler, ascended the "dragon throne". Like Kublai Khan, he wanted his power and glory to be recognized abroad. To achieve this, he determined to build a new and mighty "Treasure Fleet" of junks, and send it across the Western Sea to the great port of Calicut on India's west coast. On the way there, the fleet would stop to demand tax or "tribute" from the peoples and rulers it met, and to trade goods with them. The emperor also wanted his Treasure Fleet to tackle the dangerous pirates who lurked around the South China Sea.

Orders poured from the royal palace. Whole forests were felled inland, and their timber floated down the Yangtze River. From all over China, carpenters,

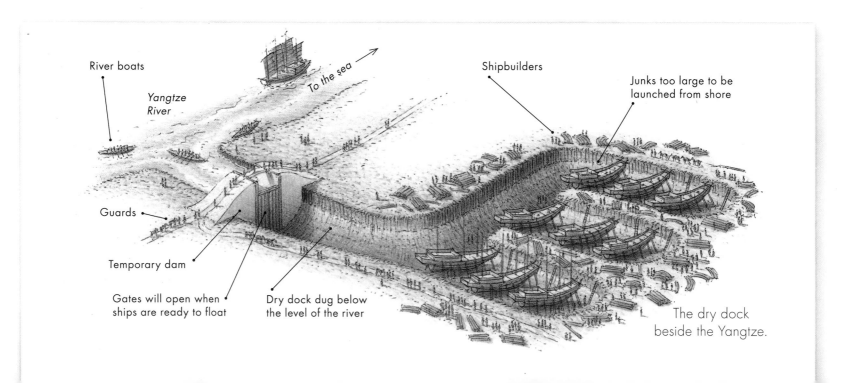

River boats

Yangtze River

To the sea

Shipbuilders

Junks too large to be launched from shore

Guards

Temporary dam

Gates will open when ships are ready to float

Dry dock dug below the level of the river

The dry dock beside the Yangtze.

sailmakers, ironsmiths and other craftsmen and their families were rounded up and moved to shipyards at Longjiang on the north-east coast.

Shipwrights set to work designing an even bigger kind of junk. The grandest vessels of the emperor's new fleet were 60 or so great treasure ships. Since none has survived, except for one broken piece of a gigantic rudder, scholars still argue over their precise size, but it seems likely that they were the largest wooden ships ever built.

For balance and stability in the water, each "super-junk" had a V-shaped hull, a long keel, stone ballast and floating anchors to hold the vessel straight in rough weather. There was plenty of room for the large crew needed to sail it, as well as luxury cabins with windows and iron-rail balconies for important passengers. Its hold was stuffed with expensive porcelain and silk to trade, and its prow painted with fierce dragon eyes to frighten away the spirits of the sea.

As well as treasure ships, the emperor's fleet consisted of horse ships which carried both animals and repair materials, supply ships packed with food for the crews, water carriers holding a month's supply of drinking water, soldiers aboard troop ships, patrol boats and warships equipped with bronze cannon (gunpowder was a Chinese invention). There were some 317 ships in all. The modern US Navy, the world's largest, boasts fewer than 300.

Who would command this remarkable fleet? The right candidate had to be a brilliant organizer. As well as for the ships themselves, he would be responsible for around 27,000 men, including ambassadors, secretaries, officials, astrologers, translators, doctors and thousands of ordinary sailors and soldiers.

The emperor chose Zheng He, a man who had already served him loyally for many years. Born into a rebel Muslim family, Zheng He had been taken prisoner at the age of ten and sent to work in the army. His intelligence and talents soon marked him out and he rose to become one of the most powerful and respected men at the imperial court. Aged 35 and standing 1.8

metres tall, he was said to have an air of great authority. Even so, he had probably never been to sea before.

By autumn 1405, all was ready. The emperor gave a lavish banquet at which prayers and offerings were made to the sailors' goddess, Tianfei, and to the ever-threatening water dragons responsible for terrible storms. *"Let the dark water dragons go down into the sea,"* ran the incantation, *"and leave us free from calamity."* When the formalities were over, the fleet slipped out of Nanjing harbour, down the Yangtze River and into the East China Sea.

Sailing in tight formation, the emperor's seaborne embassy was an extraordinary sight. Communication between the ships was a crucial but tricky business. Each craft had its own large flag. It also had bells, gongs and drums that throbbed out orders across the waves. Lanterns flashed night signals; pigeons carried longer-range messages.

The fleet sailed 650 kilometres south along the coast, and then rested at Taiping to wait for favourable monsoon winds to take it over the South China Sea to Champa, in modern-day Vietnam. There, the people bought porcelain and silk from the ships, and made gifts of prized aloe wood and ivory to the Chinese emperor.

From Champa, Zheng He sailed south to the island of Java, where he traded more porcelain and silk for local spices and copper. Here and on the coast of Sumatra, where he also stopped, he made contact with large colonies of Chinese merchants.

The narrow Straits of Malacca, through which the fleet sailed next, was a favourite haunt of pirates who preyed on the merchant ships trading between East Asia and India. Zheng He's treasure ships would have been a rich prize for any pirate captain, but they were almost impossible to capture. The fleet was heavily armed and defended. Moreover, unlike Arab or European ships of the time, the hulls of large junks were divided into watertight compartments known as bulkheads. This made them more or less unsinkable, because if water burst through the hull, three planks thick, the

THE FIRST TREASURE FLEET

Zhu Di's Treasure Fleet, represented in this picture, was the largest group of ships ever to sail under a single commander. When at sea, they would have adopted a military formation, with the warships and patrol boats encircling the more vulnerable cargo ships. The vessels communicated with each other by drum, cymbal, gong, lantern and even carrier pigeon.

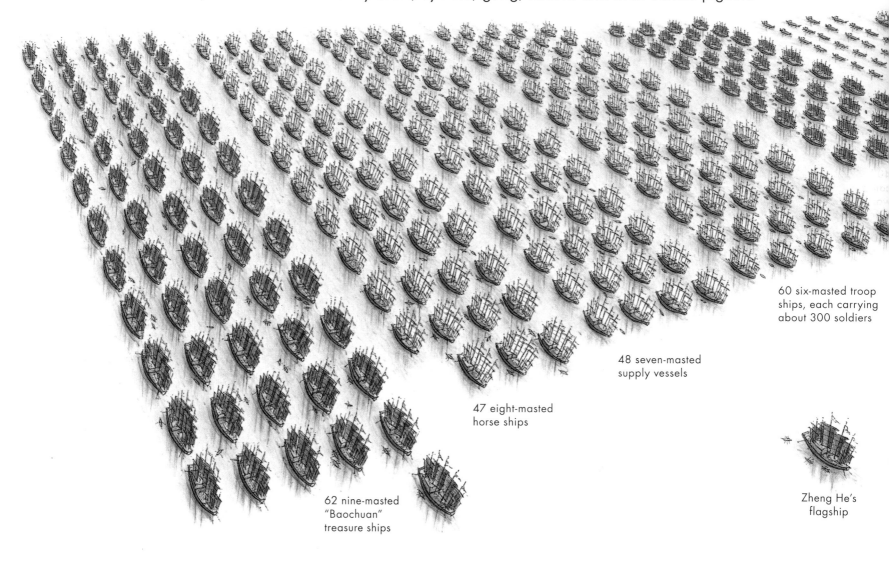

60 six-masted troop ships, each carrying about 300 soldiers

48 seven-masted supply vessels

47 eight-masted horse ships

62 nine-masted "Baochuan" treasure ships

Zheng He's flagship

bulkheads prevented it from flooding more than a single compartment. The pirates noted the fleet's size, its bronze cannon and soldiers, and left it alone. Unmolested, Zheng He took his vessels through the Straits and out into the Indian Ocean.

So far, the imperial fleet had followed the line of the coast or made only short passages over open sea. But now, crossing the ocean to Ceylon (Sri Lanka), the Treasure Fleet was far from land for several days. How did the captains navigate when out of sight of land and keep their huge ships on course?

Although they were so large, junks were surprisingly manoeuvrable. While ships in other parts of the world were steered by an oar lashed at the side, the Chinese had invented the rudder, a steering plank suspended at the centre of the stern. The ship's sail arrangement helped, too. Made of flexible silk and reinforced with bamboo batons, each linked by a rope to the hull, a junk's sails

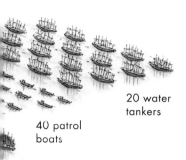

20 water tankers

40 patrol boats

40 five-masted, cannon-carrying warships known as "Fuchuan"

Scholars are unsure precisely how many treasure ships sailed with the fleet but the number was probably between 60 and 65.

were easily adjusted as the wind changed; they could also move from side to side to allow the ship to sail closer to it.

The Chinese were skilled navigators. To help them hold a steady course in a fixed direction, they used a magnetic compass. The first compasses to appear in China, toys rather than practical tools, date back to around 200 BC. Over a thousand years later, Chinese mariners had begun to use them on board ship to establish a north-south direction – setting them in small stone bowls of water to keep the needles steady at sea. Even so, Zheng He was the first person whose use of a compass for navigation is recorded in writing.

To work out how far they had sailed, the fleet's crews had to keep track of time. They did this by dividing the day into ten "watches", each counted by burning incense sticks. And to work out their latitude – how far north or south they were – they worked out the changing position of the stars above the horizon with a measuring board, known as a "qianxhingban".

In this way, they reached Ceylon. The king was not pleased to see them, however, and the fleet continued up the west coast of India to Calicut, their final destination. Here they docked for several months, exchanging their goods for jewels, coral and pepper. Eventually, in April 1407, when the monsoon winds were once again favourable, Zheng He set sail for home.

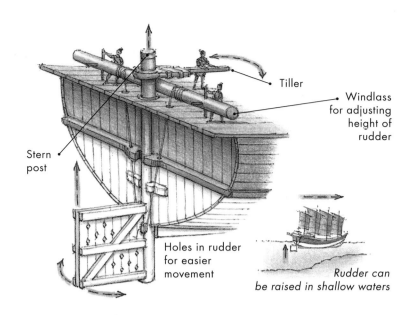

Tiller

Windlass for adjusting height of rudder

Stern post

Holes in rudder for easier movement

Rudder can be raised in shallow waters

The adjustable rudder was invented in China.

Passing through the Straits of Malacca a second time, the fleet tackled the nests of pirates who infested the region. In a campaign lasting several months, Zheng He captured their leaders and sank most of their ships.

One last adventure remained. As the fleet was re-crossing the South China Sea, a terrible storm blew up. Afraid they would be lost to the water dragons, the sailors called on the goddess Tianfei, their protector, for help. Immediately, a strange light appeared and the storm soon passed. Zheng He and his sailors took this to be a miracle. In fact, the light was St Elmo's fire,

A ship's water compass pointing north-south.

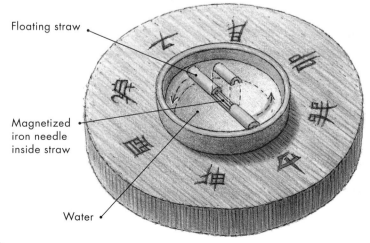

Floating straw

Magnetized iron needle inside straw

Water

ZHENG HE SETS SAILS FOR INDIA

Admiral Zheng He, commander of the Chinese imperial fleet, sailed in a "Baochuan" junk. These nine-masted triumphs of ship construction dwarfed every other vessel. Although precise measurements are unknown, they may have been over 90 metres long and 25 metres wide.

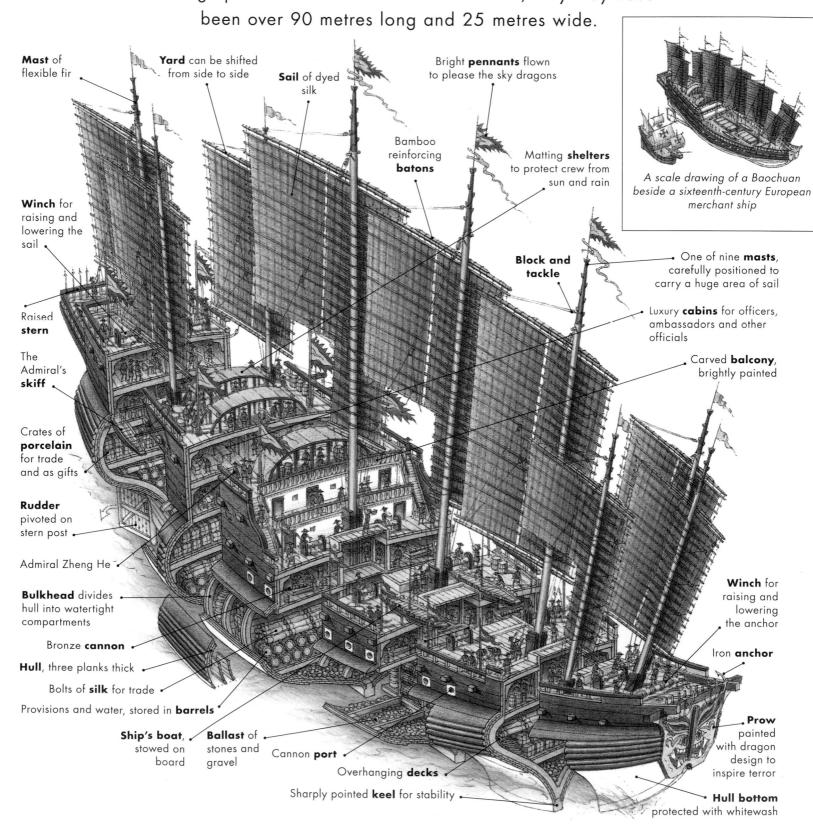

Mast of flexible fir

Yard can be shifted from side to side

Sail of dyed silk

Bright **pennants** flown to please the sky dragons

Bamboo reinforcing **batons**

Matting **shelters** to protect crew from sun and rain

A scale drawing of a Baochuan beside a sixteenth-century European merchant ship

Winch for raising and lowering the sail

Raised **stern**

The Admiral's **skiff**

Crates of **porcelain** for trade and as gifts

Rudder pivoted on stern post

Admiral Zheng He

Bulkhead divides hull into watertight compartments

Bronze **cannon**

Hull, three planks thick

Bolts of **silk** for trade

Provisions and water, stored in **barrels**

Ship's boat, stowed on board

Ballast of stones and gravel

Cannon **port**

Overhanging **decks**

Sharply pointed **keel** for stability

Block and tackle

One of nine **masts**, carefully positioned to carry a huge area of sail

Luxury **cabins** for officers, ambassadors and other officials

Carved **balcony**, brightly painted

Winch for raising and lowering the anchor

Iron **anchor**

Prow painted with dragon design to inspire terror

Hull bottom protected with whitewash

which scientists now know is caused by electricity.

After an absence of almost two years, Zheng He finally brought his ships safely home to Nanjing. The voyage had been an outstanding success. The emperor was so impressed that over the next 26 years he sent his Treasure Fleet on five more expeditions. Admiral Zheng He commanded four of them, each time sailing further and further from home – to Bengal, Persia, Oman, Yemen and Arabia. The longest voyage, lasting three years and covering 16,000 kilometres, even explored the tropical coast of East Africa.

From Kenya, the fleet brought back a giraffe as an exotic present for their imperial master. No one had ever seen this strange, gentle animal in China before. People called it a "qilin", a mythical beast that was said to appear at times of peace and prosperity. The emperor was absolutely delighted.

Zhu Di's reign ended in 1424. The Treasure Fleet's seventh and final voyage, again commanded by Zheng He, was made on the orders of Zhu Di's grandson, Emperor Zhu Zhanji. When he died, in the same year as his admiral (1435), China's age of exploration came to an end. Succeeding emperors showed little interest in the world beyond their frontiers, and the great vessels of the Treasure Fleet were left to rot quietly away. Before long, Zheng He and his extraordinary achievements were no more than a distant memory. ✪

CHINA'S
TREASURE FLEET
AMAZES the WORLD
— 1405-07 —

1. Gigantic treasure ships are built in dry dock at **Longjiang**
2. Admiral Zheng He sets sail from **Nanjing**
3. The fleet waits at **Taiping** for favourable winds
4. Trading begins at **Champa (South Vietnam)** in Indo–China
5. Zheng He meets Chinese settlers on **Java**
6. Navigating by compass, the fleet crosses the **Indian Ocean**
7. Meets hostile reception from King of **Ceylon (Sri Lanka)**
8. Destination reached: bartering the ship's cargo for Indian goods at the port of **Calicut**
9. Zheng He clears pirates from the **Straits of Malacca**
10. The returning fleet is hit by a terrible storm
11. Triumphant reception on return to **Nanjing**

CHINA

Great Wall

Zheng He

Emperor Zhu Di

JAPAN

Yangtze River

INDIA

Taiwan

PHILIPPINES

PACIFIC OCEAN

BAY OF BENGAL

SUMATRA

SOUTH CHINA SEA

BORNEO

Straits of Malacca

RIGHT AROUND THE WORLD

Searching for spice with Christopher Columbus & Ferdinand Magellan, 1492–1522

In Marco Polo's account of his travels, he talked of lush islands south of the countries he called Cathay (China) and Zipangu (Japan) *"which produce many spices ... in great abundance, particularly pepper, nutmeg and cloves"*. These were the volcanic islands of Sumatra, Java and the Moluccas or "Spice Islands", where exotic plants thrive in warm wet rainforest close to the equator. Few, if any, Europeans had ever been to them, yet they loved to use spices in all sorts of ways – to flavour food, to make perfumes and to preserve meat.

After making the long journey from Asia to Europe along the Silk Road, spices were very expensive. In the second half of the fifteenth century, prices climbed even higher, as Arab and Venetian traders faced huge new taxes imposed by the Ottoman Turks. In Venice by 1500 the cost of a kilo of pepper from Sumatra had soared to 2.5 gold ducats – the price of a small house.

Not surprisingly, Europeans began to look for a way to bypass the Silk Road. If they could only find a sea route, they would be able to send their own merchants to trade directly with oriental ports. But first, three things needed to happen: they would have to develop seaworthy ships capable of ocean crossings; they would need to

learn how to navigate away from land and they would have to discover exactly where the Spice Islands lay.

At the end of the fifteenth century, Portugal and Spain were Europe's leading sea powers. The Portuguese had begun to develop a new kind of ship: the caravel. As well as having plenty of space for its crew and cargo, the caravel could carry enough supplies for a long sea voyage. It was steered by a stern-post rudder, a Chinese invention first used by Zheng He. And it could be rigged either with traditional European square sails or with the triangular lateen sails used on Arab boats. The latter could swing easily to catch the wind, allowing a ship to tack (steer a zigzag course) into a headwind. The caravel was equipped with another Chinese invention, too: the magnetic compass. At last, European sailors – who, when out of sight of land, had previously navigated only by the stars and the sun – could steer a course under cloudy skies, by day or by night.

In these ships, Portuguese sailors began to explore. They started along the west coast of Africa. Further and further south they sailed, in a series of voyages, until, in 1488, a captain called Bartholomew Dias reached the Cape of Good Hope at the southern tip of the continent. Ten years later, following the same route, another Portuguese captain, Vasco da Gama, rounded the Cape and crossed the Indian Ocean to the great Indian trading port of Calicut, which Zheng He had visited almost a century earlier.

Meanwhile, other European sailors were interested in finding a different route to the Spice Islands. If the world was round, as the Ancient Greeks had calculated it must be, shouldn't ships be able to reach China and the Spice Islands by sailing west, too? Christopher Columbus, an experienced Italian captain from the port of Genoa, believed so. A keen reader of Marco Polo, he was sure that Zipangu and Cathay lay just across the Atlantic.

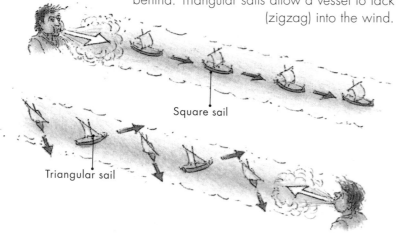

Square sails work best when the wind is blowing from behind. Triangular sails allow a vessel to tack (zigzag) into the wind.

Square sail

Triangular sail

A LATEEN-RIGGED CARAVEL

Triangular sails allowed a ship to steer much closer to the wind.

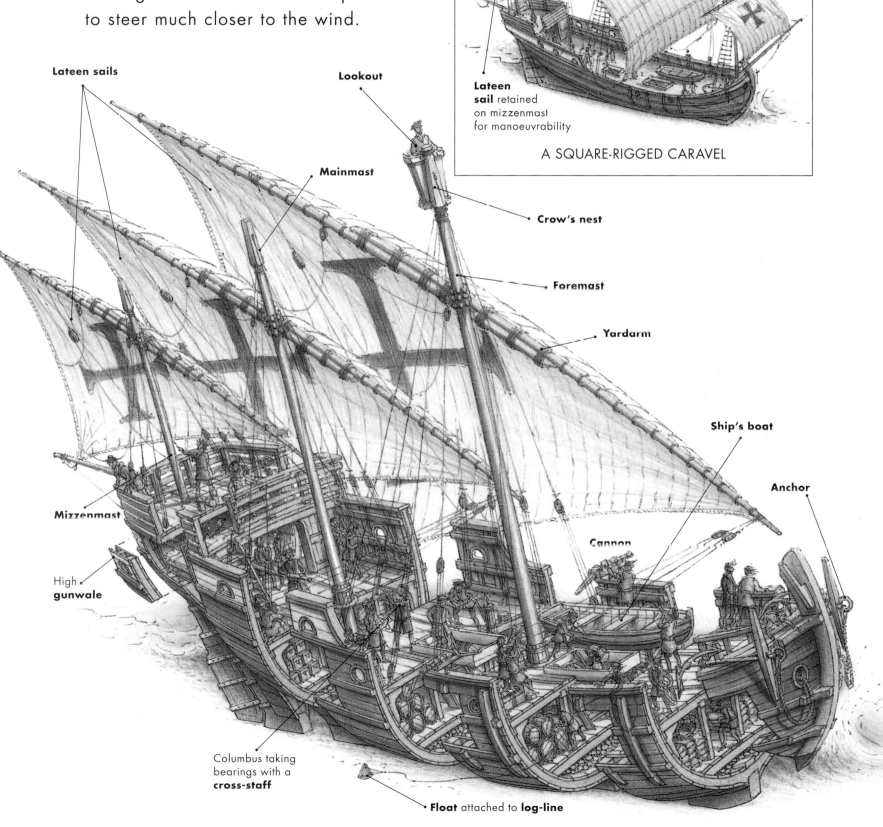

Square sails rigged for a following wind

Lateen sail retained on mizzenmast for manoeuvrability

A SQUARE-RIGGED CARAVEL

Lateen sails

Lookout

Mainmast

Crow's nest

Foremast

Yardarm

Ship's boat

Anchor

Mizzenmast

Cannon

High **gunwale**

Columbus taking bearings with a **cross-staff**

Float attached to **log-line**

For years, Columbus begged the Spanish monarchs, Queen Isabella and King Ferdinand, to back him on a westward voyage of exploration. Eventually, after much wrangling and delay, Isabella agreed. On Friday 3 August 1492, Columbus' tiny fleet of three ships set sail from the port of Palos and headed out into the Atlantic. The lateen-rigged *Niña* and *Pinta* were caravels, while Columbus' flagship, the square-rigged *Santa Maria*, was a larger ship known as a carrack, which the Portuguese had developed from the caravel.

To avoid the stormy North Atlantic, Columbus first sailed south-west to the Canary Islands, which Spain had occupied in 1483. Here he re-rigged the *Niña* and *Pinta* with square sails, so that they could take advantage of the prevailing westerly winds. On 6 September, with fresh supplies of food and water on board, he set out once more. This time the captain headed due west, into the setting sun.

The fleet made good progress, and when they had been at sea for three days, Columbus set up two logbooks. In a private one, he recorded the actual distances covered each day; in the other, which was public, he wrote down shorter distances, so the crew would believe themselves closer to home than they really were.

But nothing could prevent the sailors' alarm when they reached the floating gulfweed of the calm Sargasso Sea. They had never before seen anything like it, and thought they might not get out. To their relief, a few days later, they spotted some bosun birds, which are known

The ship's compass, suspended in a special box to keep it level, showed direction. The hourglass, which measured time, was turned over every sixty minutes.

never to fly far from land. Shortly afterwards, on the night of 11–12 October, a lookout did indeed sight land.

Columbus was sure that the delightful green island that greeted his eyes next morning lay just off the coast of Marco Polo's Zipangu. He named it San Salvador, and then hurried on in search of a mainland. Over the next few weeks, he sighted and named many more of what we now call the Caribbean islands, including Cuba and Hispaniola (Haiti). Convinced that they were all part of the East Indies (islands to the east of India), he was nevertheless mystified that the "Indian" inhabitants could tell him nothing about the Great Khan of China.

Around midnight on Christmas Day 1492, when the ship's boy was at the tiller, the *Santa Maria* ran aground on a coral reef off Hispaniola and began to fill with water. As it was impossible to float her off, Columbus had to abandon her. The disaster persuaded him to turn back to Spain to report on his discoveries so far, rather than continue exploring. But 39 members of the crew were left behind to set up a Spanish colony on the island.

The *Niña* and *Pinta* set sail for home on 16 January 1493. The prevailing winds forced them further north than on the outward voyage, and on 12 February the vessels lost sight of each other during a tremendous storm which lasted for three days. *"The ocean,"* Columbus wrote in his journal, *"was in rebellion, such that we could neither advance nor make our way out of the waves attacking the caravels."* The ships did not meet again

To find their longitude, sailors used a method called dead reckoning. This involved: (a) working out the ship's speed from a float with a knotted string or rope attached and (b) measuring with hourglasses how long they had been at sea.

until 15 March, when they both reached Palos on the same tide.

Columbus made three more transatlantic voyages of exploration. By the time of his death in 1506, he knew that he had discovered a large number of islands, as well as *"a very great continent, until today unknown"*. That continent was soon given the name by which we know it today – America. What he did not know, or even suspect, was that between this new continent and China lay the Pacific, the world's largest ocean. It was left to the expedition of a later explorer, Ferdinand Magellan, to discover that the world was a quarter larger than Columbus had estimated.

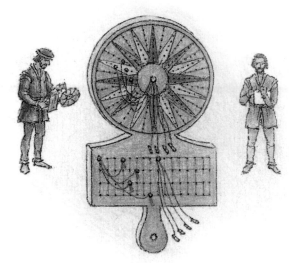

A traverse board of the type used by Magellan and Columbus to plot a straight course that allowed for the lateral movement of an ocean current.

Magellan was a Portuguese nobleman. Between 1505 and 1512 he sailed east, as far as the Indian Ocean and the Java Sea, and took part in battles and expeditions to defend Portugal's new interests in the region. He

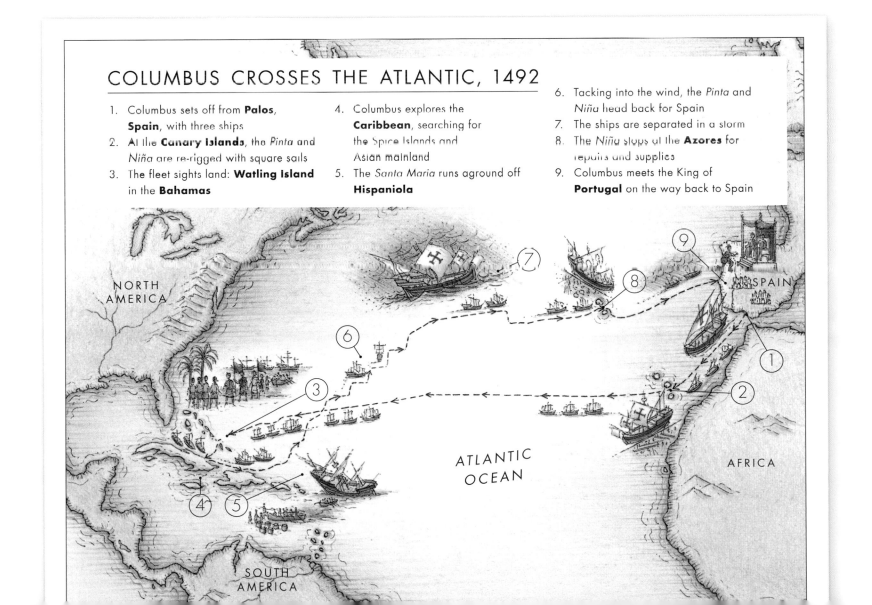

COLUMBUS CROSSES THE ATLANTIC, 1492

1. Columbus sets off from **Palos, Spain**, with three ships
2. At the **Canary Islands**, the *Pinta* and *Niña* are re-rigged with square sails
3. The fleet sights land: **Watling Island** in the **Bahamas**
4. Columbus explores the **Caribbean**, searching for the Spice Islands and Asian mainland
5. The *Santa Maria* runs aground off **Hispaniola**
6. Tacking into the wind, the *Pinta* and *Niña* head back for Spain
7. The ships are separated in a storm
8. The *Niña* stops at the **Azores** for repairs and supplies
9. Columbus meets the King of **Portugal** on the way back to Spain

NORTH AMERICA

SPAIN

AFRICA

ATLANTIC OCEAN

SOUTH AMERICA

Using an astrolabe to measure the height of the sun above the horizon in order to work out latitude. Tricky work on a rolling ship.

observer called them *"old crates; their ribs are as soft as butter"*. But they carried between them an impressive cargo of goods to trade, including 20,000 hawk bells and brass bracelets, 500 looking-glasses and many bolts of velvet. The 250 or so passengers and crew included Antonio Pigafetta, an Italian gentleman who kept a detailed diary from which he would later write a vivid account of the expedition, *Magellan's Voyage Around the World*.

Magellan sailed south down the coast of Africa, then south-west over the Atlantic at its narrowest point, crossing the equator as he went. Avoiding Portuguese territory in northern Brazil, on 13 December he anchored in Guanabara Bay (now Rio de Janeiro). Here the men repaired the ships, took on fresh supplies of food and water, and enjoyed a warm and sunny southern-hemisphere Christmas. The very next day, Magellan ordered his fleet

returned not only an experienced soldier, sailor and navigator, but also convinced that he could reach the Spice Islands more easily by sailing west, just as Columbus had thought. He believed there was a passage through South America leading to a "South Sea" on the other side. Having fallen out with the Portuguese king, he managed to persuade the new king of Spain, Charles I, to put up the money for a voyage to find it.

Magellan set sail from Spain on 20 September 1519. His fleet consisted of four carracks – the *San Antonio, Concepción, Victoria* and *Santiago* – and his flagship caravel, the *Trinidad*. The boats were far from new. In fact, one

1. Magellan sets out from **Spain**
2. The fleet reaches **Guanabara Bay, Brazil**
3. The crew overwinters at **Puerto San Julián**
4. The *Santiago* is wrecked exploring the coast
5. The *San Antonio* deserts and returns to Spain

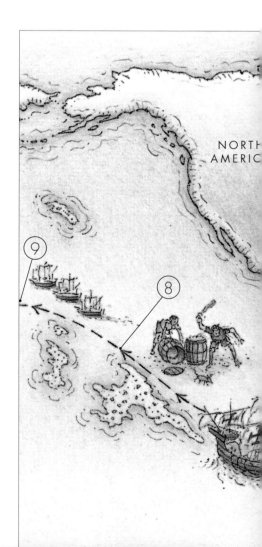

NORTH AMERICA

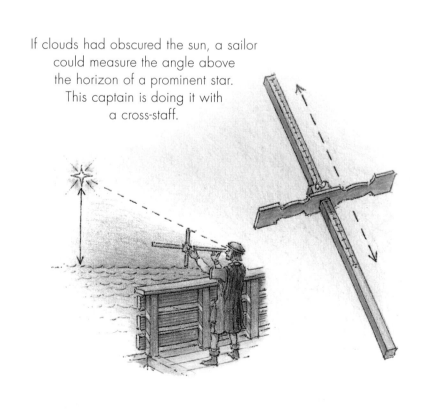

If clouds had obscured the sun, a sailor could measure the angle above the horizon of a prominent star. This captain is doing it with a cross-staff.

south again to begin the search for a channel leading to the west.

The further they sailed, hugging the rugged coastline, the colder it became and still there was no sign of a westward route. Finally, in late March, the freezing Antarctic winter closed in and Magellan ordered the fleet to drop anchor in the sheltered harbour of Puerto San Julián. Here they stayed for many months, the weather making progress impossible. It was a terrible time. Magellan had to put down a mutiny by officers who feared they would all die of cold and starvation. Then, on a reconnaissance trip, the *Santiago* was wrecked. Fortunately, all its crew was saved.

Eventually, the first signs of the southern spring appeared and on 18 October the fleet set out again. After just three days' sailing they came upon an opening between tall sheer cliffs on their starboard side. Could this be the passage they were looking for?

The crew of the *San Antonio* decided not to risk their lives finding out. Clapping their captain

MAGELLAN & ELCANO SAIL ROUND THE WORLD, 1519–22

6. The remaining three ships discover a passage through to the Pacific – the **Straits of Magellan**
7. They sail north-west in search of the Spice Islands
8. Reduced to eating rats, many of the crew perish
9. The fleet sails on across the **Pacific Ocean**
10. Land at last: the island of **Guam**. Fresh food and water after 98 days at sea
11. Magellan is slain in the **Philippines** and the remaining sailors burn the *Concepción*
12. Led by Captain Elcano, the *Victoria* and the *Trinidad* finally reach the **Spice Islands**
13. The *Trinidad* tries (unsuccessfully) to retrace its route across the **Pacific**
14. The *Victoria* heads west across the **Indian Ocean**
15. Elcano brings the leaking *Victoria* round the **Cape of Good Hope** into the Atlantic
16. The *Victoria* arrives home in **Spain**

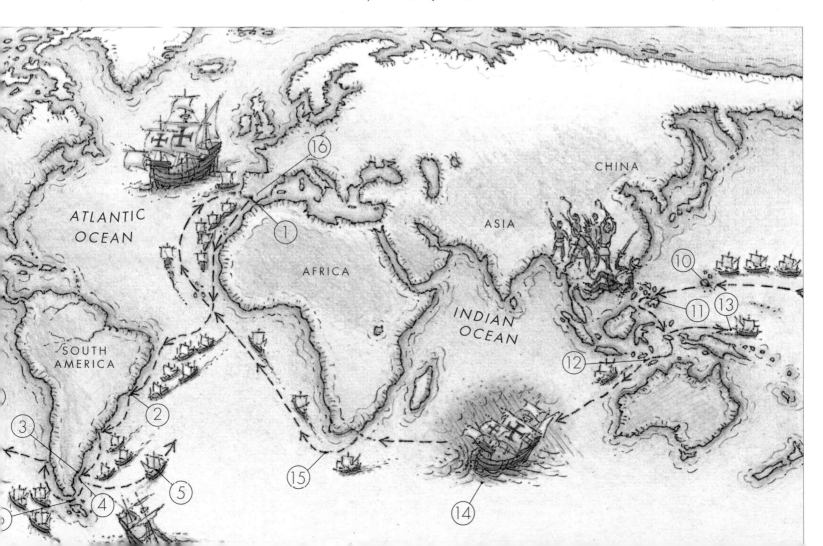

(Magellan's brother) in irons, they deserted and set sail back to Spain. The remaining three ships went on, carefully nosing their way west, along what turned out to be 537 kilometres of mazy channels and sounds that snaked between bleak mountains. At last, on 28 November 1520, they sailed into open sea on the other side. The channel that they had found has been known as the Straits of Magellan ever since.

Little did they know that the toughest part of their journey was yet to come. Magellan had had a strong hunch he would find a strait, but he knew nothing at all about the ocean he had now reached. Most important of all, he had no idea of its size. He reckoned a voyage to the Spice Islands might take a few weeks. As it turned out, his battered fleet were to sail westward for over three months, covering some 15,500 kilometres before they came across any inhabited land.

This meant, of course, that there were nothing like enough supplies on board the ships to feed the crews. Grimly, Pigafetta tells how they *"ate only old biscuit turned to powder, all full of worms and stinking of the urine that the rats had made on it... We drank water impure and yellow. We also ate ox hides... And of the rats which were sold for half an ecu apiece, some of us could not get enough."* Soon men began to die – of starvation, scurvy, exposure and exhaustion.

Yet in one respect, they were lucky. Throughout the crossing, they had unusually fine weather and did not face a single storm. This led Magellan to name the sea the Pacific – or "peaceful" – Ocean.

Finally, on 6 March 1521, the fleet reached the lush Mariana Islands and dropped anchor at the island of Guam. The exhausted crew took on desperately needed provisions of rice, fruit and fresh water before sailing to the islands now known as the Philippines. There, on 27 April, Magellan was killed in a dispute with local people. Pigafetta was heartbroken. *"The renown of so valiant and noble a captain will not be extinguished in our time ..."* he wrote, *"and that this is true is seen openly, for no other had so much natural wit, boldness, or knowledge to sail once round the world."*

After their leader's death, the fleet's remaining officers held a meeting. Down to 110 men, they decided to burn the *Concepción*, as there were not enough crew left alive to sail her. The vessel's captain, Sebastián Elcano, took over command of the *Victoria*. Determined to fulfil Magellan's mission, he now pressed on with the *Trinidad* to find the elusive Spice Islands.

The two ships wandered for a long time among the many islands in the China Sea until, on 8 November 1521, they sailed into the harbour of Tidore. The Spice Islands at last! *"Therefore we thanked God..."* wrote Pigafetta. *"It was no wonder we were so glad, for (in all) we had spent twenty-seven months, less two days, in our search for Molucca."* To their relief and delight, the sultan of the island welcomed them warmly, declaring himself a loyal friend and servant to the king of Spain.

Amazed by what they found, the crew traded their cargo for sacks of cloves and nutmeg. Then they made repairs and stocked up with food and water for the return journey. To increase the chances that at least one ship would make it home, the captains agreed to split up. The *Trinidad* headed east to the Pacific, trying to get back the way it had come; the *Victoria* sailed west, towards the Indian Ocean and the Cape of Good Hope.

Unfortunately, the *Trinidad* quickly ran into storms and, returning to the Moluccas, was captured by rival Portuguese merchants. The *Victoria* had better luck. After a perilous eight-month voyage, with pumps continuously running to keep her afloat, Elcano sailed her into Seville harbour on 8 September 1522. Only 18 of her crew were still alive – but she had made it.

"From the time when we departed from that Bay until the present," declared Pigafetta proudly, *"we had sailed fourteen thousand, four hundred and sixty leagues, and completed the circuit of the world."* He had every right to boast. The Magellan–Elcano 40,000-kilometre circumnavigation was one of the greatest journeys of exploration ever made. What's more, the precious cargo of spices was still intact in the *Victoria*'s hold. ✪

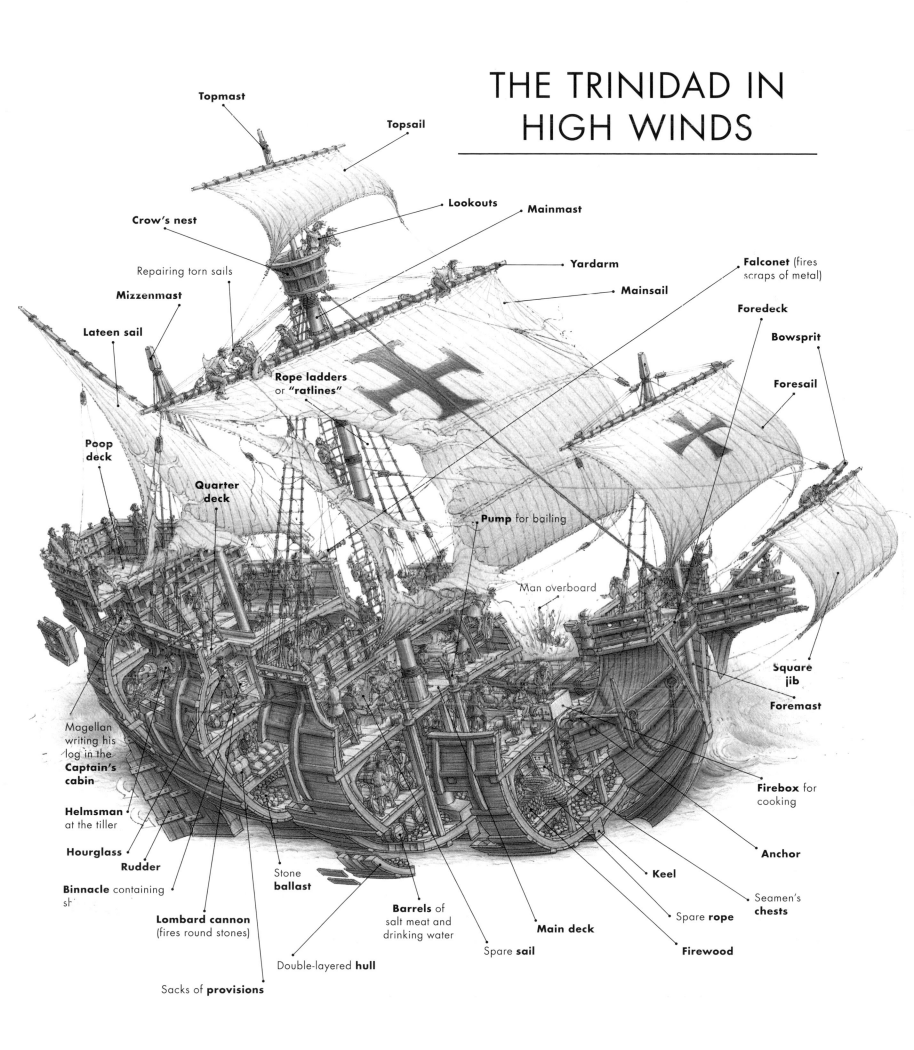

THE TRINIDAD IN HIGH WINDS

Topmast

Topsail

Crow's nest

Lookouts

Mainmast

Repairing torn sails

Mizzenmast

Yardarm

Falconet (fires scraps of metal)

Mainsail

Foredeck

Lateen sail

Bowsprit

Rope ladders or "ratlines"

Foresail

Poop deck

Quarter deck

Pump for bailing

Man overboard

Square jib

Foremast

Magellan writing his log in the **Captain's cabin**

Firebox for cooking

Helmsman at the tiller

Hourglass

Rudder

Anchor

Stone **ballast**

Keel

Binnacle containing sh

Seamen's chests

Lombard cannon (fires round stones)

Barrels of salt meat and drinking water

Spare **rope**

Main deck

Spare **sail**

Firewood

Double-layered **hull**

Sacks of **provisions**

A SOUTHERN CONTINENT?

Captain Cook maps the Pacific Ocean, 1768–71

Two hundred and fifty years after Magellan had sailed across the Pacific, very little more was known about it. There were plenty of rumours, though. One of the most widespread was of a vast and undiscovered "Terra Australis", or southern continent, lying somewhere around 40° south.

When Dutch sailors came across the fringes of New Holland (as they called Australia) and New Zealand in the seventeenth century, they thought these lands might be at the north-east corner of the mysterious continent. Geographers argued that such a land mass must exist to "balance" the large land masses of the northern hemisphere and so help the Earth spin smoothly on its axis. (The discovery of a North and South America seemed to confirm this theory.)

The man who solved the mysteries of the Pacific and produced the first accurate chart of that ocean was a superb sailor, James Cook. Self-taught in mathematics, he had worked first as a shop boy and then as a merchant seaman before joining the Royal Navy in 1755. By the age of 40, he had become a skilled navigator, charter and geographer. An ideal candidate, then, to command a joint venture between the Navy and a group of leading scientists who formed the Royal Society.

In eighteenth-century Europe, scientists were making progress in understanding the movements of the stars and planets. But no one had yet worked out how to measure the earth's exact distance from the sun. Edmund Halley, a well-known astronomer, found a solution. Every 120 years, the planet Venus can be seen passing across the face of the sun. Halley realized that the distance from the earth to the sun could be worked out mathematically if the time taken by a "transit of Venus" could be accurately measured; this would need to be done from at least two points on the earth's surface, as far apart as possible.

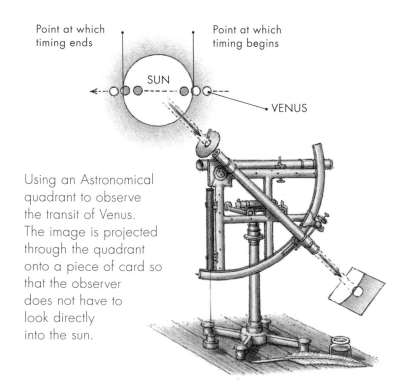

Point at which timing ends

Point at which timing begins

SUN

VENUS

Using an Astronomical quadrant to observe the transit of Venus. The image is projected through the quadrant onto a piece of card so that the observer does not have to look directly into the sun.

The next transit of Venus was due on 3 June 1769 and the Royal Society wanted to send a ship to observe it from the recently discovered King George's Island (Tahiti) in the middle of the Pacific Ocean.

The Navy agreed to provide the expedition with a ship, HM Bark *Endeavour*, and a leader, James Cook. They were less interested in science than in searching for the undiscovered southern continent without a rival nation knowing about it. They issued Cook with secret instructions to sail from Tahiti, once the transit was over, and explore the southern reaches of the Pacific Ocean. If he found no new land, he was to sail west and investigate the coast of New Zealand.

For its part, the Royal Society supplied the expedition with a portable observatory to put up on Tahiti. It also provided scientists, including the wealthy Joseph Banks, a young naturalist, whose fare helped to pay for the whole voyage. As well as many nets and specimen containers, Banks brought along stacks of books, several servants, two assistants, two artists and a pair of pet greyhounds.

What sort of ship was the *Endeavour*? Surprisingly, she was a refitted coal ship. Magellan would have been startled by her size. At 400 tonnes, she was three times as heavy as a carrack, twice as long (32 metres) and a third wider (9 metres). What would have surprised him most, though, was her flat bottom. In the North Sea, where she had worked, many dangerous sandbanks lie just below the surface. The *Endeavour* had a "shallow draught" (not much hull below the waterline) so that she could remain upright if she got stuck on the bottom. As it turned out, this would also prove useful when she was sailing over the coral shoals of the Pacific.

With 94 men on board, the *Endeavour* set sail on 26 August 1768. Her first port of call was the Atlantic island of Madeira, where she took on fresh food and water. Cook, who cared deeply about the men under his command, gave orders that they eat daily helpings of pickled cabbage and fresh fruit and vegetables whenever available. He believed that diet probably played a significant part in fending off disease. Scurvy, which doctors now know is caused by a lack of vitamin C, used to ravage crews on long voyages, including that of Magellan's expedition. But not one member of the *Endeavour* died of scurvy – though Cook had to set an example by eating large helpings of pickled cabbage himself before his men would touch it.

Crossing the Atlantic, the *Endeavour* took two months to reach the Brazilian port of Rio de Janeiro. The local authorities were suspicious of the expedition, refusing even to let Banks ashore to collect plant samples. So, after making necessary repairs and taking on fresh provisions, they set off down the east coast of South America. Cook decided not to risk the perilous Straits of Magellan. Instead, on 26 January 1769, in unusually fine weather, the *Endeavour* rounded Cape Horn at the tip of the continent and entered the Pacific.

Throughout the voyage, Cook found his ship's position by daily readings of latitude (the distance north or south of the equator) and longitude (the distance east or west of a known point). For hundreds of years, sailors had known how to calculate latitude, but calculating longitude was far trickier because it required measuring the passage of time. No one yet had invented a clock that could keep accurate time in rough seas, so Cook used a new method of calculating longitude, called lunar distances, which used the night sky as a gigantic clock. It was more accurate than dead reckoning (used by Magellan and Columbus) but still very complicated.

The party reached Tahiti on 13 April, in plenty of time for the transit of Venus. Cook and the expedition's astronomer, Charles Green, set about choosing a suitable spot for their observatory. They built a small fort round it to protect the instruments from the astonished Tahitians. The crucial day, 3 June, dawned clear and bright and the party was able to make observations that eventually led to the calculation of an accurate Earth–Sun distance.

Cook next followed his secret instructions and headed south in search of the supposed Southern Continent.

In freezing and tempestuous weather, he patrolled at 40° south. Finding no land, he headed north and then west, until the appearance of weed, seals and birds suggested they were near land. On 6 October 1769, the *Endeavour* sighted the north-east coast of New Zealand.

Charting as he went, Cook spent six months circumnavigating New Zealand, discovering it to be two islands. He then sailed 2,000 kilometres west across the Tasman Sea until, on 19 April 1770, he sighted the coast of New Holland (Australia). Ten days later the *Endeavour* anchored in a broad bay and everyone went ashore. Banks and his party collected so many plant specimens that Cook named the place Botany Bay.

But as they proceeded north along the coast, their progress slowed as they entered the Great Barrier Reef. Then, on 11 June, disaster struck when a sharp piece of coral pierced the hull and prevented the *Endeavour* from moving. In desperation, Cook ordered all non-essential heavy materials to be thrown overboard. Into the sea went ballast, guns, stores and even most of the drinking water. At the same time, everyone – including the captain – took turns at the pumps to clear the water leaking into the bilges. Eventually, a day later and some 50 tonnes lighter, the *Endeavour* floated free.

Now there was a new problem – water gushing in through the holes made by the coral. The pumps could not cope and the ship sank lower and lower in the water. The crew tried another desperate measure: fothering. This involved sewing bits of wool and untwisted rope

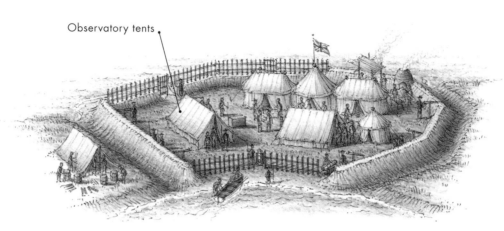

Observatory tents

The *Endeavour*'s base on Tahiti from which the transit of Venus was observed on 3 June 1769. The fortified camp was accessible only by sea.

onto an old sail and sliding it under the ship's hull, like a gigantic scarf. It worked. The wool and rope were sucked into the holes and, as Cook reported, *"our leak was so far reduced that instead of gaining upon three pumps, it was easily kept under with one"*.

Mightily relieved, Cook guided his damaged vessel into an estuary he named Endeavour River and ran the ship aground on the sloping shore. For seven weeks, the expedition's carpenters and blacksmiths carried out emergency repairs, while Banks and his party explored inland. As well as gathering hundreds more plant samples, they came across large numbers of *"an animal something less than a greyhound, [which] was of a Mouse Colour very slender made and swift of foot ... it bears no sort of resemblance to any European Animal I ever saw"*. It was, of course, the kangaroo.

With a fresh wind blowing steadily from the south, Cook had no choice but to continue sailing the patched-up *Endeavour* up the coast. Treacherous as the coral shoals were, he judged it safer to continue north than to risk a passage to open water through the *"vast foaming breakers"* crashing into the reef to his east. So it was that Cook charted Australia's entire north-east coast, going where no large ship had ever sailed before.

Finally, in August, Cook reached the Torres Strait, a passage of water that lies between Australia and New Guinea. Turning west towards Java, he confiscated all logbooks and journals and made the crew swear not to tell anyone about the places they had

CALCULATING
LONGITUDE
BY LUNAR DISTANCES

Cook used the lunar-distances method to measure his longitude. It works like this:

a Longitude is measured from an imaginary line that runs from pole to pole. This is 0° longitude.

b As the earth spins 360° every 24 hours, it spins 15° in one hour. So one hour's difference in time between two places means they are 15° of longitude apart.

c To work out his ship's longitude, therefore, Cook needed to know the precise time difference between where the boat was and the time at 0°.

A quadrant for measuring angles

d This was done by measuring the angles between the moon, which moves, and stars, which do not.

e These angles are the same everywhere on Earth. But the time at which a specific angle occurs differs according to one's longitude.

f Using a book of tables, Cook could read off his time from the angles he had measured.

g The almanac also told him what the time would be at 0° and the difference between the two gave him his longitude.

A nautical almanac

The line of 0° longitude runs through the Royal Observatory at Greenwich, London

The changing angles between the moon, which moves, and a fixed star are known as lunar distances

The almanac was based on lunar distances measured at Greenwich (0° longitude)

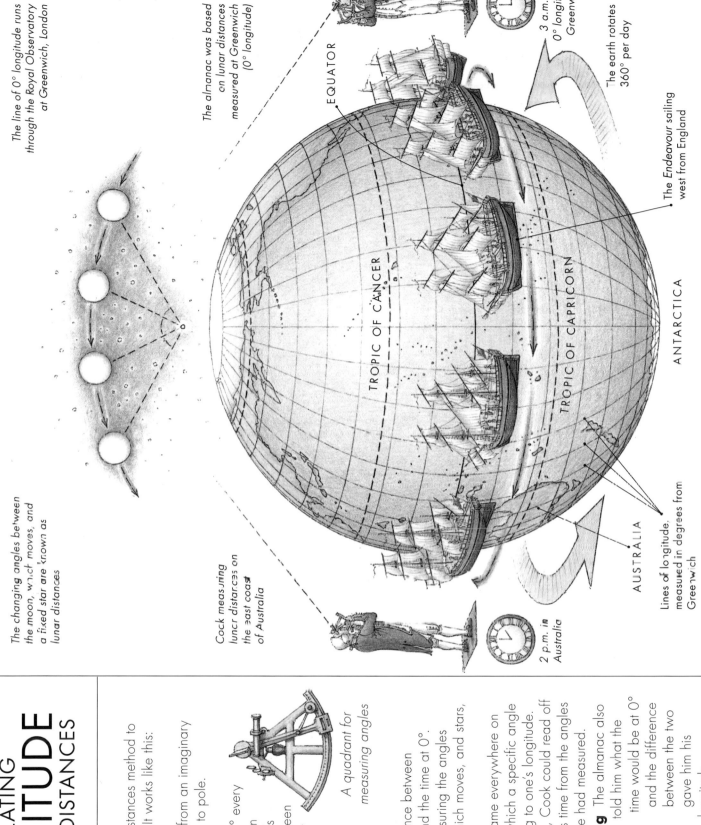

EQUATOR

TROPIC OF CANCER

TROPIC OF CAPRICORN

AUSTRALIA

ANTARCTICA

Cook measuring lunar distances on the east coast of Australia

3 a.m. at 0° longitude, Greenwich

The earth rotates 360° per day

The Endeavour sailing west from England

Lines of longitude measured in degrees from Greenwich

2 p.m. in Australia

CHARTING THE COASTS OF NEW ZEALAND AND AUSTRALIA

1. Rounding New Zealand's **North Cape**
2. Blown off course by storms
3. Confrontation with Maori warriors
4. First sighting of Australia: **Point Hicks**
5. Lands at **Botany Bay**
6. Sailing up the east coast of **Australia**
7. Navigating the **Great Barrier Reef**
8. Runs aground on coral shoal
9. Emergency repairs
10. Through the **Torres Strait**

AUSTRALIA

TASMANIA

TASMAN SEA

NORTH ISLAND

SOUTH ISLAND

NEW ZEALAND

s working aloft,
ng on foot ropes known
rses"

gallant sail

ore-topsail

Fore-course sail, the lowest and largest sail

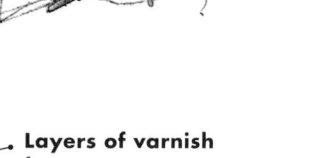

Bowsprit

Layers of varnish for protection

Wales: a raised and tarred ridge of planks

Bluff bows not designed for speed

HM BARK
ENDEAVOUR CROSSING THE TASMAN SEA

Having failed to locate a great Southern Continent and charted the coast of New Zealand, Cook heads west to try to find the east coast of the land that Abel Tasman (a Dutch captain) had called New Holland.

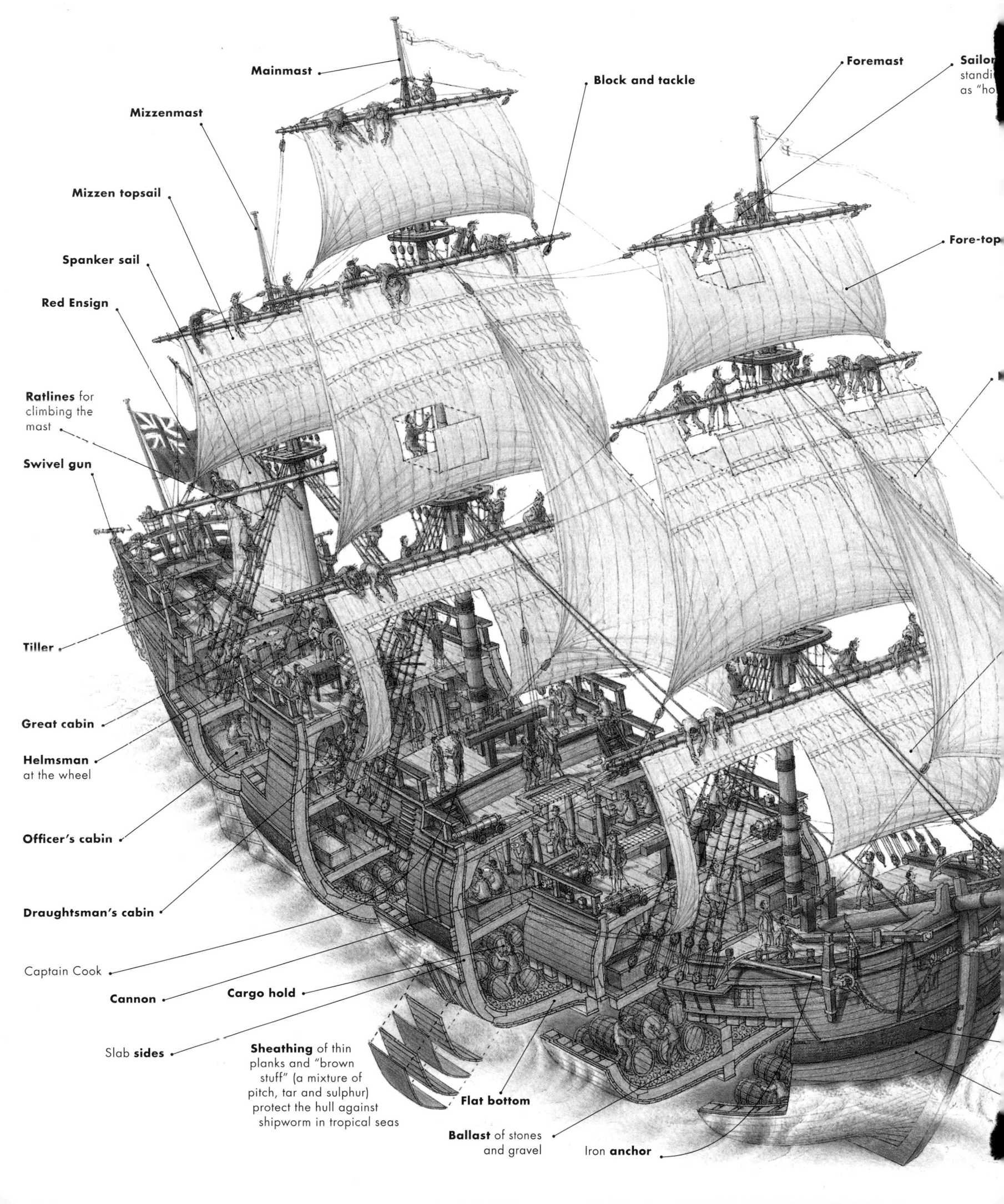

Mainmast

Mizzenmast

Mizzen topsail

Spanker sail

Red Ensign

Ratlines for climbing the mast

Swivel gun

Tiller

Great cabin

Helmsman at the wheel

Officer's cabin

Draughtsman's cabin

Captain Cook

Cannon

Slab **sides**

Sheathing of thin planks and "brown stuff" (a mixture of pitch, tar and sulphur) protect the hull against shipworm in tropical seas

Flat bottom

Ballast of stones and gravel

Iron **anchor**

Block and tackle

Foremast

Fore-top

Sailor standing as "ho

Cargo hold

REPAIRING THE *ENDEAVOUR*

Cook supervises the careening and repairs to HM Bark *Endeavour* after she has been holed by coral on the Great Barrier Reef.

High Tide

1 The *Endeavour* is hauled as far as possible up the riverbank to examine the damaged area of the hull.

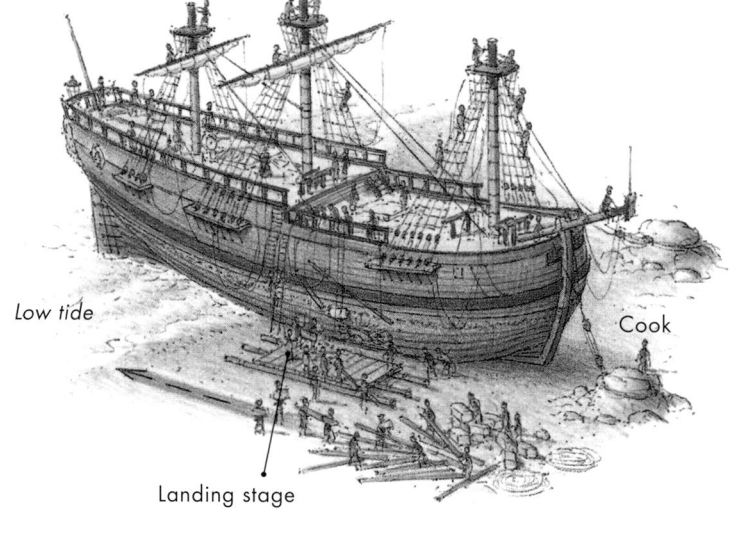

Low tide

Cook

Landing stage

2 At low tide, the masts and rigging are dismantled and the timber is used to create a landing stage. To make the ship as light as possible, the cargo and ballast are removed.

been. At Batavia (Djakarta), he docked his ship so it could be careened.

All but three of the men on board were in good health when they arrived. But on land they were exposed to diseases for which there was not yet any cure – malaria and dysentery. By the time Cook set out for home 12 weeks later, seven men had died, 40 were sick and *"the rest of the ship's company were in a very feeble condition"*. As they crossed the Indian Ocean towards the Cape of Good Hope, in a *"ship that was nothing better than a hospital"*, a further 23 men died.

Nearly three years after setting out, on 10 July 1771 the *Endeavour* sighted southern England. Two days later, crew and passengers came ashore and the epic voyage ended. The expedition's discoveries were a blow to those who believed in the existence of a Southern Continent. But they did not give up all hope. It took a second voyage (1772–75), in which Cook circumnavigated the world twice at latitudes never previously attempted, for doubters finally to accept

that Australia really was the only large continent in the southern Pacific. ✪

Harrison's chronometer: This clock was the first to keep time accurately on board a moving ship. It enabled Cook to work out his longitude quickly and easily on his second and third voyages.

Low tide

Patching the hole

High tide

3 The crew haul on ropes to careen (tip over) the ship, exposing the damage. The hull is then patched, cleaned and tarred.

4 At high tide, the ropes are released and the ship returns to an upright position. Once the cargo and ballast are back on board, she is refloated with the aid of 38 empty barrels.

COOK'S CIRCUMNAVIGATION, 1768–71

1. HM Bark *Endeavour* leaves **Plymouth**
2. Provisioning at **Madeira**
3. Minor repairs at **Rio de Janeiro**
4. Rounding **Cape Horn**
5. Joseph Banks collects plant specimens on the way to Tahiti
6. At **Tahiti** for the Transit of Venus
7. Searching for a great Southern Continent
8. Charting the coast of **New Zealand**
9. Aground on the **Great Barrier Reef**
10. Many die of disease at **Djakarta**
11, 12, 13. The voyage home

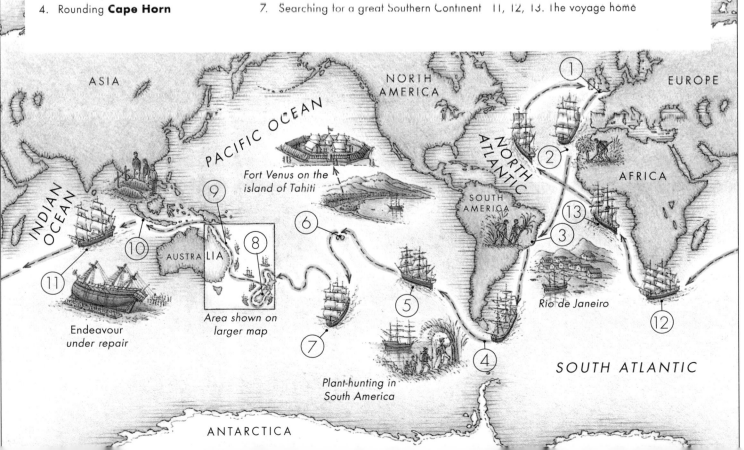

ASIA

NORTH AMERICA

EUROPE

PACIFIC OCEAN

Fort Venus on the island of Tahiti

NORTH ATLANTIC

AFRICA

INDIAN OCEAN

SOUTH AMERICA

AUSTRALIA

Area shown on larger map

Endeavour under repair

Rio de Janeiro

Plant-hunting in South America

SOUTH ATLANTIC

ANTARCTICA

INSIDE AFRICA

Steaming upriver with David Livingstone, 1858–64, and Mary Kingsley, 1895

The world's second largest continent never needed "discovering". Traders from the Middle East had been operating along its east coast since the time of the pharaohs, while the Portuguese and other Europeans had been exploring and settling its west coast for several centuries. But until the nineteenth century, few outsiders knew anything at all about Africa's vast interior.

Among the earliest Europeans to show an interest in Africa beyond its shores was Joseph Banks, the botanist who had sailed with Captain Cook. Many others were inspired by him, including the Scottish doctor and missionary David Livingstone. Between 1854 and 1856, Livingstone made the first recorded east–west journey across the continent – from Luanda, on the coast of modern-day Angola, to Quelimane, on the coast of modern-day Mozambique. On his return, he wrote a bestselling book, *Missionary Travels*, in which he described a country quite different from that which his readers had imagined. Instead of bare arid desert, he wrote of rich tropical forests, lush plains and spectacular rivers like the Zambezi. Europeans learned for the first time about the Zambezi's Mosi-oa-Tunya Falls, which Livingstone was the first Westerner to see. (Patriotically, he called them the Victoria Falls, after his distant queen.)

Livingstone was strangely silent about the river's angry hippopotamuses, hungry crocodiles and malaria-carrying mosquitoes. Moreover, in spite of these dangers, he was anxious to return to the Zambezi. He believed that if he could prove it was navigable, it might become a *"highway into the interior"* and open the continent up to trade. If successful commerce were established, it would compete with and even wipe out the inhumane slave trade. For centuries, outsiders had been taking Africans prisoner and sending them to the Americas, the Caribbean and the Middle East to work as slaves. Although Britain had made slavery illegal in 1833, the doctor was disgusted to discover that other countries continued to practise it.

The nineteenth century was the great age of steam. In 1769, James Watt (another Scotsman) had patented an early design for a steam engine. Gradually, as the technology developed, steam engines came to power all sorts of things, from mill and factory machinery to railway trains and even ships.

The ship that brought Livingstone back to East Africa in May 1858 was a 48-metre steamer called the *Pearl*. On it, in kit form, were the pieces of a smaller river-going paddle steamer named *Ma Robert* (after Mrs Livingstone, whose eldest son was called Robert). The British government had built it especially for the explorer, who was now a celebrity. Livingstone's plan was to sail the *Pearl* 418 kilometres upriver to the town of Tete, unloading stores along the way.

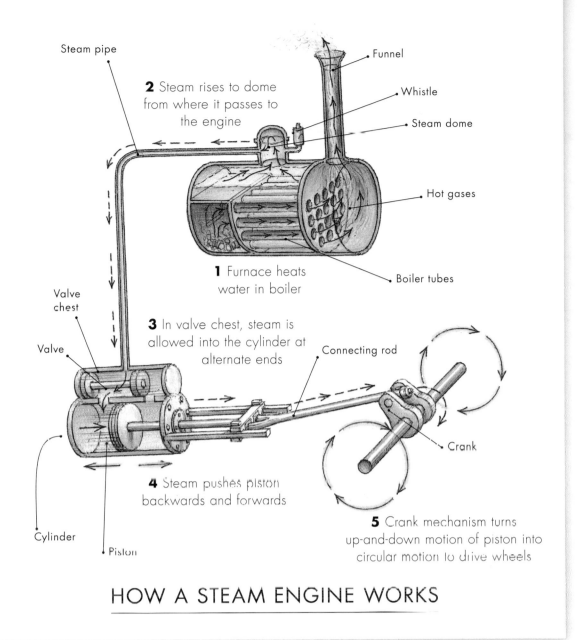

2 Steam rises to dome from where it passes to the engine

Steam pipe

Funnel

Whistle

Steam dome

Hot gases

1 Furnace heats water in boiler

Boiler tubes

Valve chest

3 In valve chest, steam is allowed into the cylinder at alternate ends

Valve

Connecting rod

Crank

4 Steam pushes piston backwards and forwards

Cylinder

Piston

5 Crank mechanism turns up-and-down motion of piston into circular motion to drive wheels

HOW A STEAM ENGINE WORKS

was too deep for travel as far as Tete. Livingstone and his party had to transfer to the *Ma Robert* sooner than expected. Laden with more stores than she had been built to carry, the little steamer was forever grounding on sandbanks. In temperatures of 38°C, dragging her off with ropes and winches was exhausting work for her crew, many of whom now had malaria.

Worse was to come. It was soon clear that the *Ma Robert* had serious design faults. Her engine was not powerful enough to drive her upstream against strong currents, and her boiler consumed vast quantities of wood: a day's steaming needed one and a half day's woodcutting. Her hull was made of thin sheets of a new kind of steel that had not been tested. It soon developed so many holes that it leaked like a colander and had to be continually pumped out. *"For us steam was no labour-saving power,"* Livingstone grumbled in his journal. He called the *Ma Robert* all sorts of names: *"the wretched little steamer"*, the *"tin kettle"* and *"the slow puffing Asthmatic"*. It probably did not help that while he was an able geographer and navigator, he was not – unlike Cook or Magellan – much of a sailor.

Living conditions on the vessel were awful. Cockroaches bred quickly in the warm dark hold and swarmed everywhere. The mood on board became gloomier and gloomier. Finally, just 225 kilometres beyond Tete, the leaking boat met with an obstacle that no technology could overcome:

They would then sail back to the river's mouth, and the expedition would continue up the Zambezi, beyond Tete, in the *Ma Robert*. Livingstone was accompanied by six others: Dr James Kirk, a botanist; Richard Thornton, a geologist; Thomas Baines, a watercolour painter; George Rae, an engineer; Norman Bedingfeld, a naval officer; and Charles Livingstone, his brother.

When they arrived at the mouth of the Zambezi, Livingstone was in good spirits. Government support, a strong team and a brand-new river steamboat would surely make the expedition a success. But almost at once, things began to go wrong. The Zambezi turned out to be shallower than he had anticipated, with many sandbanks and shifting channels. The *Pearl's* draught

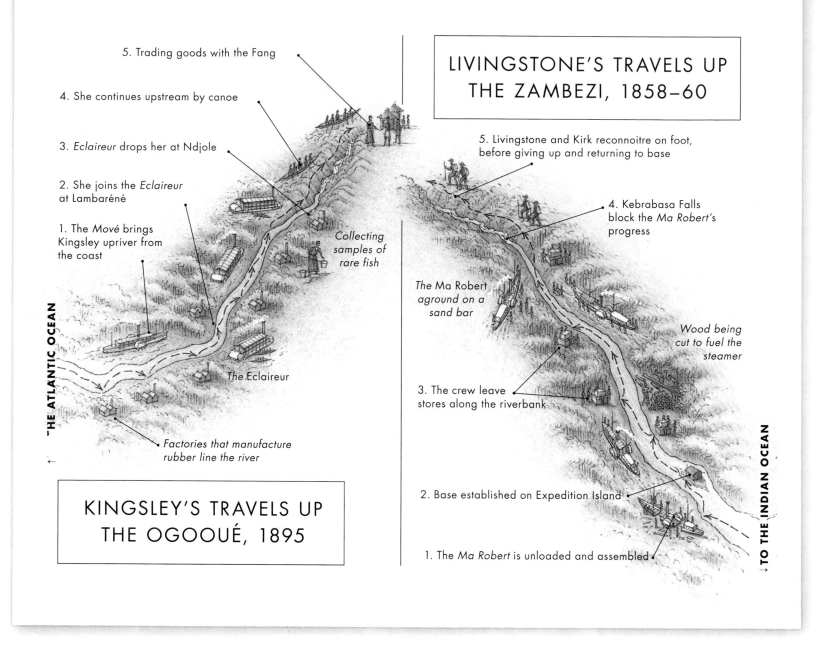

5. Trading goods with the Fang

4. She continues upstream by canoe

3. *Eclaireur* drops her at Ndjole

2. She joins the *Eclaireur* at Lambaréné

1. The *Mové* brings Kingsley upriver from the coast

Collecting samples of rare fish

The Eclaireur

THE ATLANTIC OCEAN

Factories that manufacture rubber line the river

KINGSLEY'S TRAVELS UP THE OGOOUÉ, 1895

LIVINGSTONE'S TRAVELS UP THE ZAMBEZI, 1858–60

5. Livingstone and Kirk reconnoitre on foot, before giving up and returning to base

4. Kebrabasa Falls block the *Ma Robert*'s progress

The Ma Robert aground on a sand bar

Wood being cut to fuel the steamer

3. The crew leave stores along the riverbank

2. Base established on Expedition Island

1. The *Ma Robert* is unloaded and assembled

TO THE INDIAN OCEAN

25-metre-high waterfalls in the Kebrabasa Gorge formed an impassable barrier.

The Kebrabasa Falls forced the expedition to turn back. Undaunted, Livingstone decided to explore the Shire River, a tributary of the Zambezi, and mapped the wonderful Lake Nyasa at its head. Nevertheless, the British government regarded the expedition as a failure and recalled it in 1864.

Just over 30 years later, in 1895, a very different sort of explorer landed on the west coast of Africa. Mary Kingsley was an Englishwoman travelling alone. She carried a waterproof sack packed with blankets, books, a bowie knife and revolver, hairpins and the clothes she wore whether she was in Africa or in London –

The fearless Mary Kingsley shoots the Alemba Rapids on the Ogooué.

THE MA ROBERT

A Scottish shipbuilding company, Lairds, built this little paddle steamer especially for Livingstone's exploration of the Zambezi. Delivered in kit form and assembled in Africa, the vessel was a failure, owing to her many design faults.

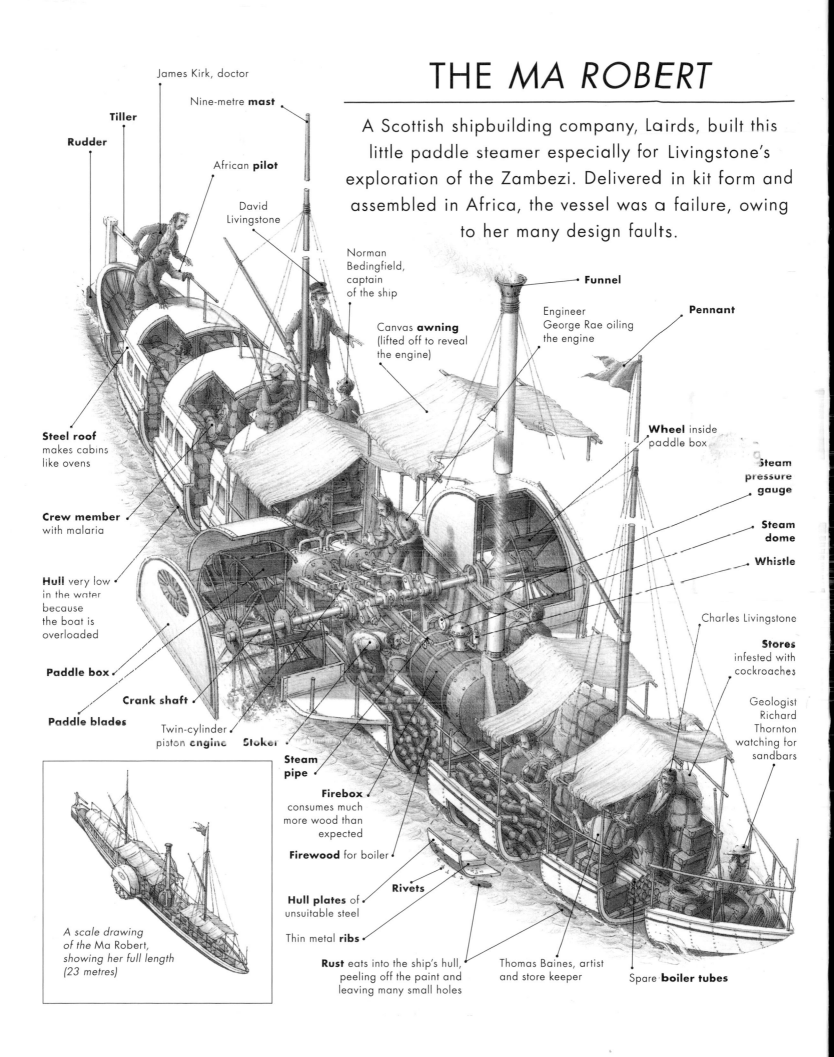

James Kirk, doctor

Nine-metre **mast**

Tiller

Rudder

African **pilot**

David Livingstone

Norman Bedingfield, captain of the ship

Canvas **awning** (lifted off to reveal the engine)

Funnel

Engineer George Rae oiling the engine

Pennant

Steel roof makes cabins like ovens

Wheel inside paddle box

Steam pressure gauge

Steam dome

Crew member with malaria

Whistle

Hull very low in the water because the boat is overloaded

Charles Livingstone

Stores infested with cockroaches

Paddle box

Crank shaft

Geologist Richard Thornton watching for sandbars

Paddle blades

Twin-cylinder piston **engine**   **Stoker**

Steam pipe

Firebox consumes much more wood than expected

Firewood for boiler

Rivets

A scale drawing of the Ma Robert, showing her full length (23 metres)

Hull plates of unsuitable steel

Thin metal **ribs**

Rust eats into the ship's hull, peeling off the paint and leaving many small holes

Thomas Baines, artist and store keeper

Spare **boiler tubes**

MARY KINGSLEY BOARDS THE ECLAIREUR AT LAMBARÉNÉ

210 kilometres from the sea, Mary Kingsley joins a flat-bottomed river steamer ferrying passengers and goods deep into the heart of Gabon.

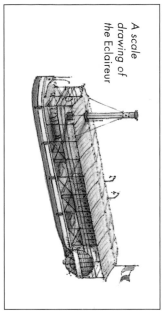

A scale drawing of the Eclaireur

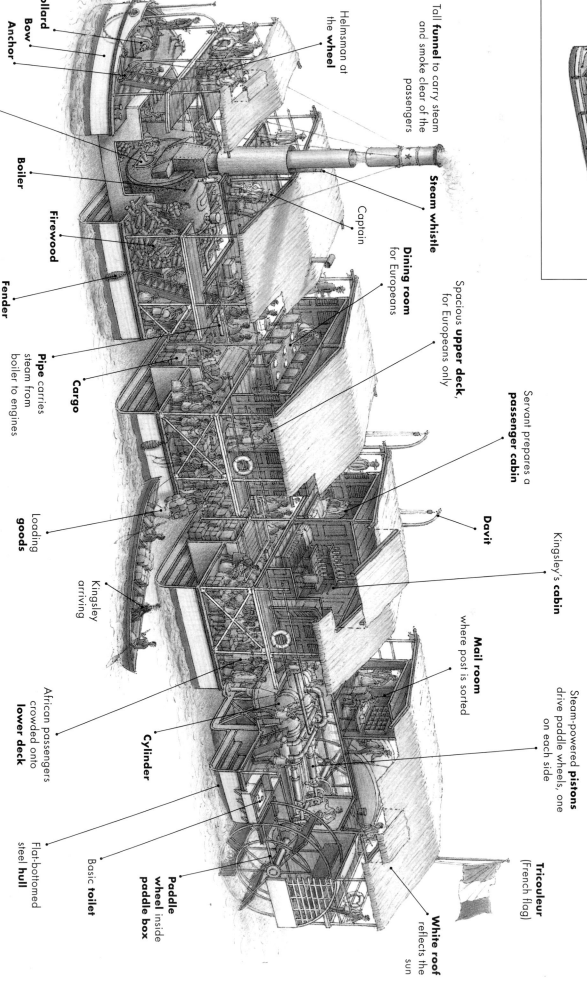

Bollard

Bow

Anchor

Stoker feeds the **firebox**

Boiler

Firewood

Fender

Pipe carries steam from boiler to engines

Cargo

Loading **goods**

Kingsley arriving

African passengers crowded onto **lower deck**

Cylinder

Basic **toilet**

Flat-bottomed steel **hull**

Paddle wheel inside **paddle box**

Helmsman at the **wheel**

Tall **funnel** to carry steam and smoke clear of the passengers

Steam whistle

Captain

Dining room for Europeans

Spacious **upper deck**, for Europeans only

Servant prepares a **passenger cabin**

Davit

Kingsley's **cabin**

Mail room where post is sorted

Steam-powered **pistons** drive paddle wheels, one on each side

White roof reflects the sun

Tricouleur (French flag)

long black skirts, white cotton blouses and black leather boots. Her luggage also included a medical bag and a case stuffed with specimen bottles for rare fish she hoped to collect, as well as toothbrushes, glass beads, wire fish hooks, cloth and tobacco to trade with as she went.

Her plan was to travel as far as she could up the great brown Ogooué River which winds 1,110 kilometres into the heart of Gabon. As a keen zoologist (a student of animal life), she hoped to discover new species of insect and freshwater fish. And as an anthropologist (someone who studies the different ways groups of human beings behave), she planned to spend time with the Fang tribe, many of whose villages lay in the remote interior. To overcome the questions that were bound to arise from her travelling alone, she proposed to trade her way. *"When you first appear among people who have never seen anything like you before,"* she wrote, *"they naturally regard you as a devil; but when you want to buy or sell from them, they recognize there is something human and reasonable about you."*

How would she travel upriver? By now, paddle-wheel steamers regularly journeyed as passenger ferries along African rivers. On the morning of 5 June, Kingsley set off from the port of Glass on the *Mové*, a French paddle steamer with a wood-burning boiler. By now steam technology had greatly improved and Mary found her *"a fine little vessel"*.

The *Mové* steamed south along the coast, crossed the equator in the afternoon, and reached the broad mouth of the Ogooué by evening. Chugging steadily upriver, over the next two days the steamer carried Kingsley between banks of overhanging forest to the small settlement of Lambaréné, 210 kilometres from the sea. From here, she waited to catch a small stern-wheel steamer, the *Éclaireur*, bound for Ndjole, 150 kilometres upstream, which she reached on 23 June.

Kingsley was now entering what she called the *"raw Africa"* that she liked best. As no passenger boats ventured further up the Ogooué, she taught herself to handle a dug-out canoe – an extremely difficult skill – and paddled her way further and further inland. Trading as she went, she was always a cause of astonishment in villages where no European woman had been seen before. In search of a new species of fish, she also braved the *"majestic, singing dance"* of a thunderous waterfall called the Alemba Rapids. Her frail craft was tossed about like a twig, but somehow she survived.

Kingsley made other journeys to Gabon to study her beloved Fang tribe, travelling through country that Europeans had not visited before. She was one of only a handful of women explorers of her time, and on her return to Britain she recounted her experiences to packed halls. The book she published in 1897, *Travels in West Africa*, has never been out of print. Her sympathy and warmth for Africa did much to dispel ignorance about a continent that was still little understood and consequently feared. ◉

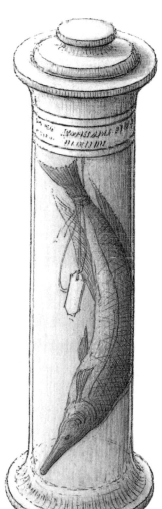

One of 65 species of fish that Kingsley brought back from Africa, three of which bear her name.

OVER THE NORTH POLE

Umberto Nobile flies across the Arctic, 1928

For most of history, explorers travelled by land or sea. Although their journeys would have been easier by air, human beings learned to fly only quite recently. The story began in November 1783, when the Montgolfier brothers sent two volunteers 150 metres above Paris in a hot-air balloon. They landed safely 25 minutes later.

By watching the fire burning in his grate, the inventor Joseph Montgolfier had realized that warm air rises because it is lighter than colder air around it. His flying machine put this principle into practice. It worked by burning a fire beneath a huge cloth bag. When this bag, or "ballon", filled with warm light air, the whole contraption lifted off the ground with a basket suspended beneath it.

Not long after the Montgolfier flight, a physicist, Jacques Charles, filled a balloon with hydrogen gas, which is 93 per cent lighter than air. It flew 25 kilometres in 45 minutes. Helium gas, which is less flammable than hydrogen, was found to work too, and by the mid-nineteenth century, ballooning had become a craze. The wealthy flew for sport and for pleasure, and in 1862, two scientists, James Glaisher and Henry Coxwell, made studies of the upper atmosphere in a balloon that rose over 10,000 metres.

But there was a difficulty. Balloons could not be steered and went only where the wind took them, which often led to crashes. In the early twentieth century, engineers tackled the problem by developing the "dirigible", a French word meaning "able to be steered".

Also known as airships, dirigibles were huge cigar-shaped balloons with a cabin hanging underneath. There were two types. Rigid ones had a lightweight metal frame inside that allowed the balloon to hold its shape when it was not inflated. Semi-rigid ones collapsed when not inflated, having only a metal keel along the bottom to which the cabin was fixed. Both kinds had propeller engines to drive them forwards, and movable fins at the back for steering.

Airships did not have the skies all to themselves. In 1903, the brothers Wilbur and Orville Wright made the first aeroplane flight at Kitty Hawk in North Carolina, America. Unlike a balloon, their plane was heavier than air. It flew because, when pulled forward by motor-driven propellers, its wings lifted it up. Early aeroplanes were fast but quite unreliable and unable to fly long distances. Airships were slower but could fly non-stop for thousands of kilometres. At first, many aeronauts preferred them, especially for travel over water.

Twentieth-century explorers were quick to see that flight would be an effective way to discover more about the frozen wildernesses of the Arctic and the Antarctic. The first journeys to the poles had been made on foot, or on sleds pulled by dogs. In 1909, an American party led by Robert Peary claimed to be the first to reach the North Pole. Two years later, a Norwegian expedition, led by Roald Amundsen, crossed the Antarctic to the South Pole. Both men returned to tell their tale, but many polar explorers did not.

In 1925, Amundsen got in touch with Umberto Nobile, an Italian engineer who designed semi-rigid dirigibles. The following year, the two men set off for the Arctic in the airship *Norge*. They flew from the northernmost tip of Norway, right across the North Pole to Alaska. Their journey set two records: it was the first undisputed flight over the North Pole, and it was the first flight to cross the Arctic from Europe to North America. The explorers also proved that there was no land mass at the North Pole, only frozen ocean.

After his success with the *Norge*, Nobile was keen to return to the Arctic as soon as he could. Backed by

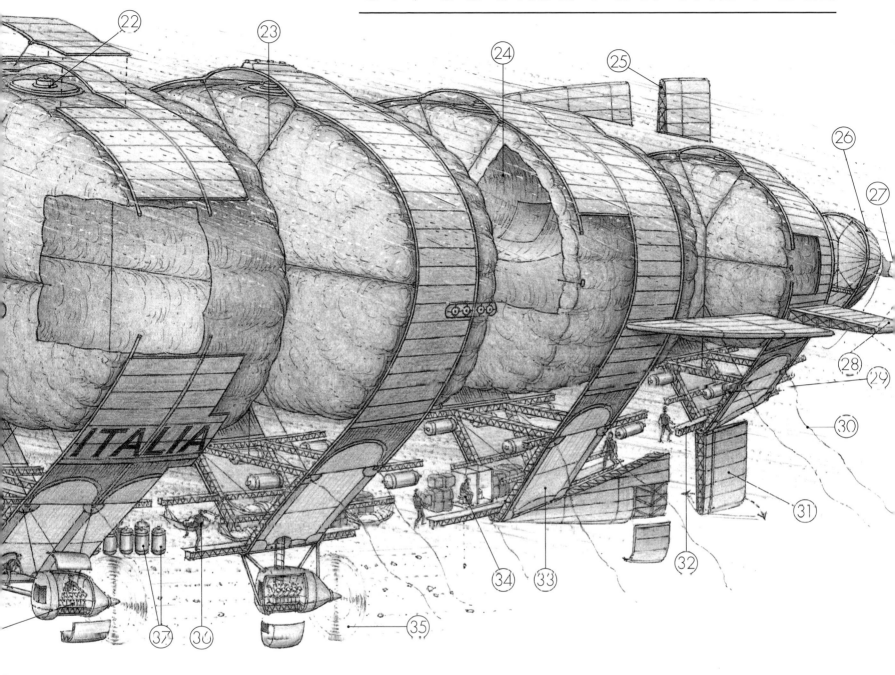

20. **Engineer**
21. 250-horsepower Maybach **engine** in pod
22. Ballonet **valve**
23. Bracing **wires** hold gas bags in place
24. Small **airbag** inside the ballonet allows hydrogen to expand and contract
25. Honeycomb **fin** structure
26. **Tail**
27. **Tricolore** (Italian flag)
28. **Rudder flap** steers ship up and down

29. Triangular **keel**
30. **Mooring rope**
31. **Rudder flap** steers left and right
32. **Catwalk** runs the entire length of the semi-rigid airship
33. Thick **rubber strips** protect the lower envelope from flying ice
34. **Toilet**
35. **Propellers** spit out shards of ice
36. **Hammock**
37. Petrol **tanks**

the Royal Geographical Society of Italy, he planned five research flights over the North Pole and northern Greenland in a new, improved airship, the *Italia*. Among its crew of 16 were navigators, technicians, engineers, scientists, radio operators and a meteorologist. Nobile brought his beloved pet terrier, Titina, too.

Early on the morning of 15 April 1928, the *Italia* rose into the air above Milan. As well as crew, she was carrying 1,360 kilograms of equipment, nearly 4,000 kilograms of fuel and around 1,800 kilograms of ballast. On the 5,150-kilometre journey north, she battled hail, snow, fog, heavy winds, ice and lightning, but landed safely at King's Bay base camp on the remote island of Spitsbergen, deep within the Arctic Circle.

From here, on 11 May, Nobile set off on the first of his research flights. He planned a daring voyage across Greenland to the mouth of the Mackenzie River in northern Canada. But violent snowstorms forced him to abandon the trip, and eight hours after take-off the *Italia* was back at King's Bay.

Four days later, Nobile set off for Nicholas II Land (now called Severnaya Zemlya). The weather was fine and he and the crew were able to chart and photograph 48,000 square kilometres of unknown Arctic Ocean. Though strong winds blew the *Italia* southwest of its final destination, the trip was a success.

On 23 May, Nobile set out on an even more ambitious journey. He hoped to drop a team of scientists at the North Pole to investigate the temperature and nature of seawater beneath the ice cap. The *Italia* would fly on to explore Greenland's northern coast and pick up the scientists on her way home.

For the first eight hours, all went well. Visibility was good and wind speeds low. Then conditions worsened. A swirling mist enveloped the airship, which was also

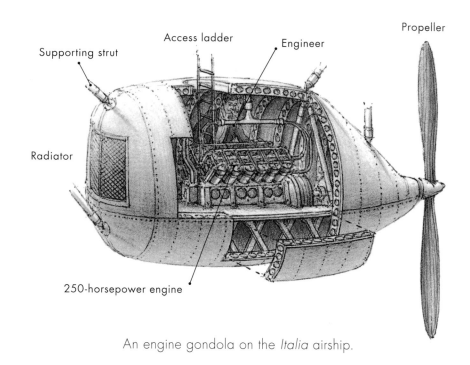

An engine gondola on the *Italia* airship.

being chased by a strong tail wind. Knowing he could not land a party of men there now, Nobile pushed on for the Pole anyway.

At 24 minutes after midnight on 24 May, he reached it. Circling low, he dropped onto the snow a large oak cross – wrapped in an Italian flag – which the Pope had given him. Giuseppe Biagi, a radio operator, sent a message back to the Italian government. Despite the danger they were in, the crew were in triumphant mood.

Their high spirits did not last long. For the next 24 hours, as the *Italia* tried to fly back to King's Bay, she struggled to make headway against gales that brought in rolling fog and heavy snow. Ice formed on her propellers, then flew off in shards that pierced the hull. The crew filled the holes as best they could with cement, but then the steering froze, sending the airship nose-diving towards the ice below. Just in time, Nobile gave the order to cut the engines, and the *Italia* began to rise. One thousand metres up she went, through the storm clouds into the sunlit skies above.

Precisely what happened next is unclear. Heated by

ANATOMY OF AN AIRSHIP

Capable of flying enormous distances (far greater than any aeroplane of the time), the *Italia* had one major downside: its size and buoyancy meant that it was easily blown off course in high winds.

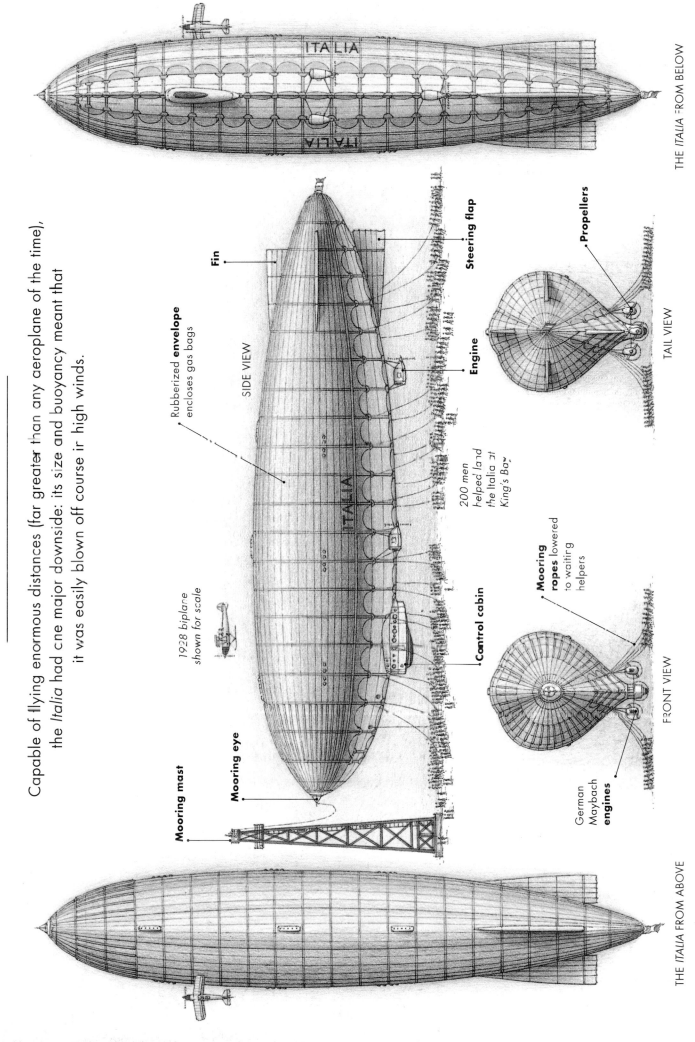

THE *ITALIA* FROM BELOW

Rubberized **envelope** encloses gas bags

Fin

Steering flap

SIDE VIEW

Engine

TAIL VIEW

Propellers

1928 biplane shown for scale

200 men helped land the Italia at King's Bay

Mooring ropes lowered to waiting helpers

Control cabin

German Maybach **engines**

FRONT VIEW

Mooring mast

Mooring eye

THE *ITALIA* FROM ABOVE

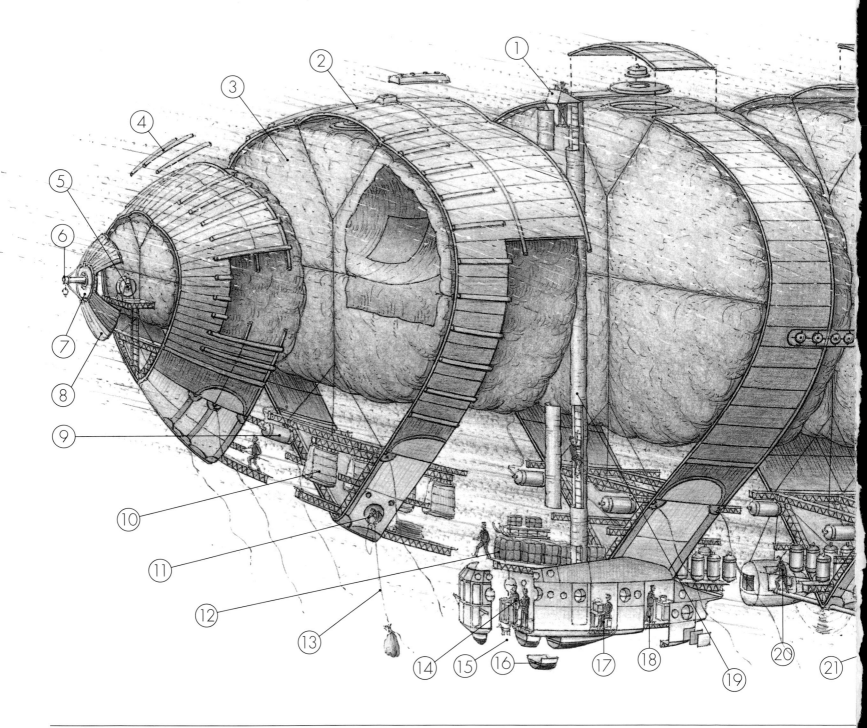

KEY

1. **Observation post**
2. **Envelope** of rubberized cloth
3. **Ballonet**: hydrogen-filled gas bag, made from the intestines of oxen
4. Steel **reinforcement strips**
5. **Bow winch**
6. **Mooring eye**
7. **Window** for docking at mooring mast
8. **Nose**
9. Liquid-hydrogen **tank**

10. **Ballast bags** filled with water
11. Anchor-line **port**
12. Ballast bags and **supplies**
13. Weighted **ground-anchor line**
14. **Control cabin** with Nobile at the controls
15. Titina, Nobile's dog
16. **Pneumatic skid** absorbs the shock of landing
17. **Radio operator**
18. **Kitchen** with hot and cold running water
19. **Access shaft** to observation post

the warmth of the sun, the hydrogen in the airship's envelope expanded. Safety valves released some of it, so that the envelope would not burst. But when the *Italia* came back down to resume her journey, it seems that too much gas had been released and she was too heavy to stay airborne. Down, down, down she fell, until she crashed heavily into the ice.

One engine and the control cabin smashed off, throwing Nobile and nine others out headlong. One man was killed and four, including Nobile, were badly injured. Five others were unharmed – as was Titina, the dog. And what of the stricken *Italia*? The survivors watched in horror as, dragged along by the raging gale, the wreck of the enormous airship disappeared into a blanket of driving snow with six men still on board. They were never seen again.

Fortunately for the survivors, chief engineer Ettore Arduino had tossed fuel, food and camping equipment from the *Italia* before it vanished. What's more, Biagi had held on tight to his emergency radio during the crash. Now he rigged up an aerial and coaxed the set to life, broadcasting, *"SOS Italia..."* Finding some red dye among their supplies, the crew daubed it over their tent to make it more visible to search aircraft. It was all a matter of time: if they were not found soon, summer fogs would hinder visibility from the air, and the ice floe on which they were marooned would start melting away.

As it turned out, the search for the *Italia*'s stranded crew took many weeks. It involved six nations, 18 ships, 22 aeroplanes and 1,500 men. Tragically, more people died in the rescue operation – including Amundsen, who flew from Norway but was never seen again – than had been killed in the crash. When eventually the tiny red tent was spotted, Nobile was lifted from the ice, not in one of his beloved airships but in an aeroplane. The era of exploration by airship was over. ✪

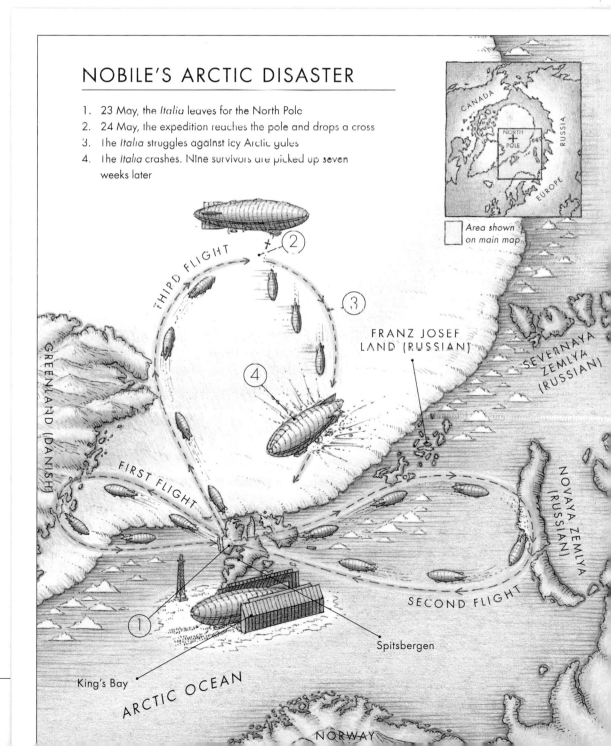

NOBILE'S ARCTIC DISASTER

1. 23 May, the *Italia* leaves for the North Pole
2. 24 May, the expedition reaches the pole and drops a cross
3. The *Italia* struggles against icy Arctic gales
4. The *Italia* crashes. Nine survivors are picked up seven weeks later

CANADA
RUSSIA
NORTH POLE
EUROPE

Area shown on main map

THIRD FLIGHT

FRANZ JOSEF LAND (RUSSIAN)

SEVERNAYA ZEMLYA (RUSSIAN)

GREENLAND (DANISH)

FIRST FLIGHT

NOVAYA ZEMLYA (RUSSIAN)

SECOND FLIGHT

Spitsbergen

King's Bay

ARCTIC OCEAN

NORWAY

THERMOSPHERE
*Scorchingly hot:
12 x boiling point,
32 x human body
temperature*

Outer space

MESOPAUSE
*Temperatures here
can fall to -100°C*

*Around
85 kilometres up*

MESOSPHERE
*Temperatures as low
as the lowest ever
recorded on Earth*

STRATOPAUSE
*Temperatures can
rise to 0°C*

*Around
50 kilometres up*

STRATOSPHERE
*Not enough air
for breathing and
temperatures as cold
as at the poles*

TROPOPAUSE
Completely dry

*Around
15 kilometres up*

TROPOSPHERE
Wet and oxygen-rich

*The surface of
the earth*

THE LAYERS OF EARTH'S ATMOSPHERE

ABOVE AND BELOW

The Piccards soar to the stratosphere and plunge to the Mariana Trench, 1932–60

By the early 1930s, explorers had travelled to every corner of the earth, and mapped nearly all its land surface. Some said there was nowhere new to go. However, many remote places remained that had not yet been visited. Who knew, for example, what lay in the stratosphere, that vast blue canopy above the clouds, the traditional realm of angels? Or what lurked in the depths of the deepest, darkest oceans? Were there monsters there?

Manned balloon flights had already risen to the lower reaches of the stratosphere, and recently invented submarines had dived 300 metres or more below the surface of the sea. But such journeys were extremely dangerous. The air is so thin in the stratosphere that there is not enough oxygen for breathing, and human bodies collapse. Equally terrible, in deep seas, water may weigh a crushing 1.23 tonnes per square centimetre, enough to squash an ordinary submarine like an empty drink can.

One family faced these dangers – and triumphed. Auguste Piccard and his son Jacques were among the bravest explorers of all time. Unlike adventurers of the past, they were not steely soldiers or hardy mariners; rather, they were scientists. Swiss-born Auguste Piccard (1884–1962) studied engineering in Zurich before becoming a professor of physics in Brussels, Belgium. There he grew interested in new theories about the cosmic rays that were believed to be active in the stratosphere. To learn more, he decided to go and observe them directly.

In those days, the stratosphere was beyond the reach of any aeroplane, so the only way to travel there was by balloon. In 1862, scientists James Glaisher and Henry Coxwell had risen over 10,000 metres in a balloon. In

1912, Victor Hess, the scientist who discovered the existence of cosmic rays, had reached over 5,000 metres. But all three had nearly died in the process. So how could Piccard ascend to 12,200 metres, as he hoped, and still return safely to Earth?

Backed by Belgium's Fonds National de la Recherche Scientifique (National Fund for Scientific Research), Auguste constructed a remarkable balloon. Its enormous canopy was made from very light cotton, sealed with a thin coat of rubber. To make it rise, the canopy was inflated with lighter-than-air hydrogen, as Nobile's airship the *Italia* had been. To descend, the crew pulled a cord to release hydrogen from the top of the canopy, making the whole balloon heavier.

Below the canopy hung a lightweight aluminium sphere. This specially designed cabin, with eight tiny portholes and two hatches, was just large enough for a two-man crew and their instruments. Once the balloon had risen to 1,500 metres, the hatches were sealed and the cabin became air-tight, so the pressure inside remained constant no matter how high the balloon went. (The same principle applies to the pressurized cabins that are standard on all modern high-flying passenger aircraft.) In order for Piccard and his assistant to breathe safely, the cabin was equipped with around ten hours' supply of pure oxygen and a system for recycling stale air.

On 26 May 1931, the *FNRS* (the balloon was named after its sponsor), lifted off from Augsburg, Germany. Up and up and up it went, climbing into the stratosphere. Amazingly, some 17 hours later, it floated safely down again and landed in the Swiss Alps. On this first flight, Piccard and his assistant, Paul Kipfer, had reached a world-record 15,785 metres. However, an air leak and the tangling of the hydrogen-release valve had made it too dangerous to gather any scientific data.

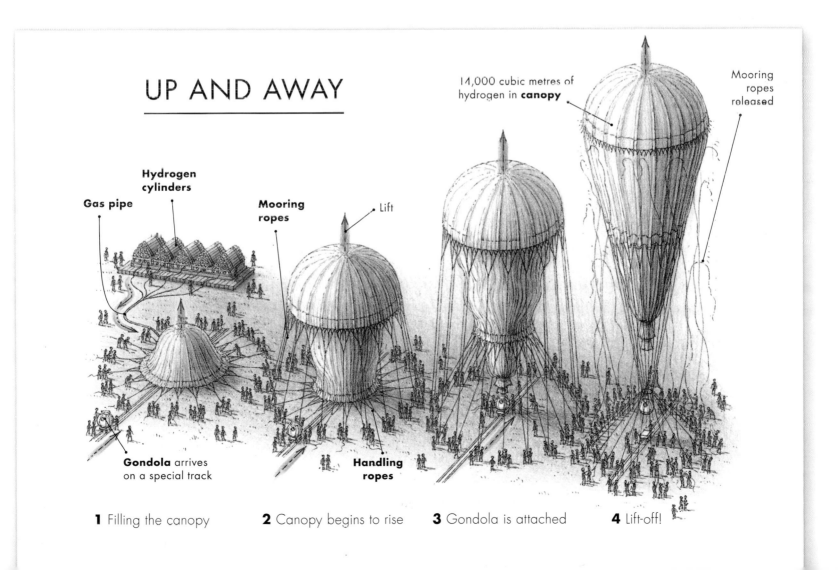

UP AND AWAY

Hydrogen cylinders

Gas pipe

Mooring ropes

Lift

14,000 cubic metres of hydrogen in **canopy**

Mooring ropes released

Gondola arrives on a special track

Handling ropes

1 Filling the canopy   **2** Canopy begins to rise   **3** Gondola is attached   **4** Lift-off!

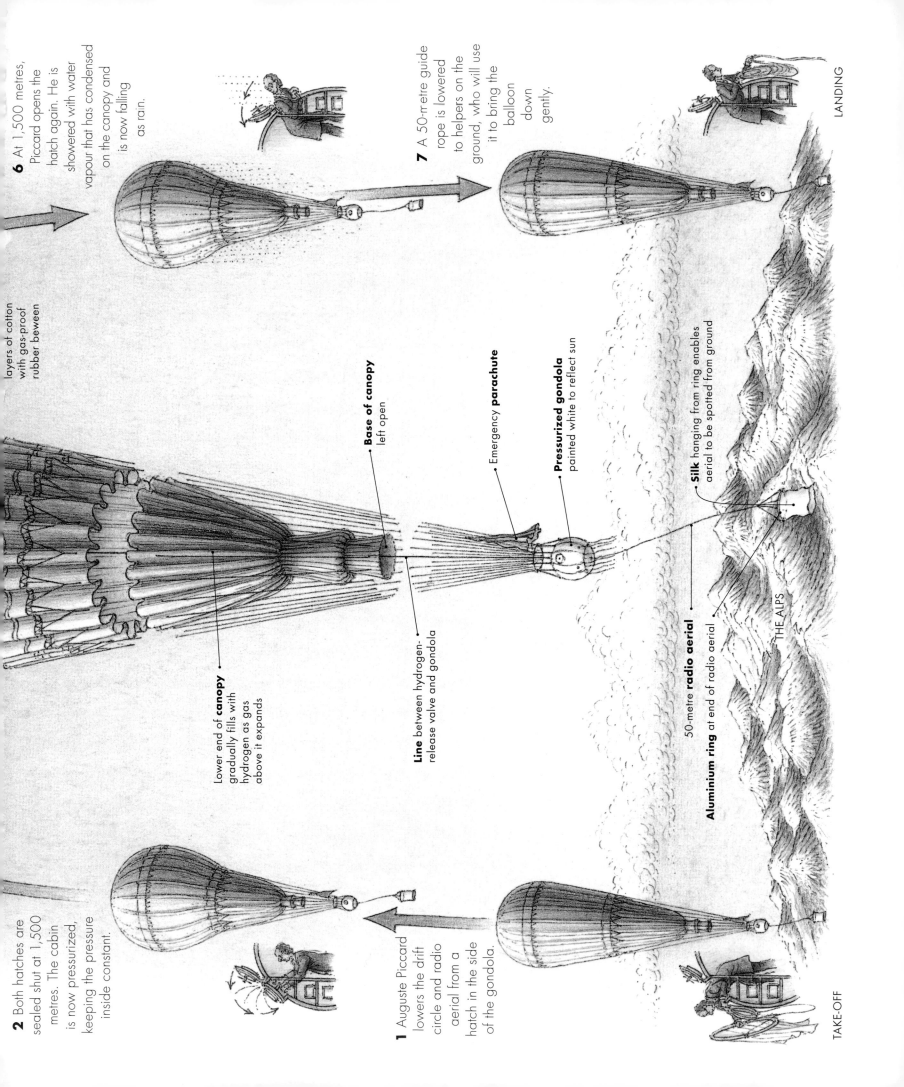

6 At 1,500 metres, Piccard opens the hatch again. He is showered with water vapour that has condensed on the canopy and is now falling as rain.

7 A 50-metre guide rope is lowered to helpers on the ground, who will use it to bring the balloon down gently.

LANDING

layers of cotton with gas-proof rubber beween

Base of canopy left open

Emergency **parachute**

Pressurized gondola painted white to reflect sun

Silk hanging from ring enables aerial to be spotted from ground

Lower end of **canopy** gradually fills with hydrogen as gas above it expands

Line between hydrogen-release valve and gondola

50-metre **radio aerial**

Aluminium ring at end of radio aerial

THE ALPS

2 Both hatches are sealed shut at 1,500 metres. The cabin is now pressurized, keeping the pressure inside constant.

1 Auguste Piccard lowers the drift circle and radio aerial from a hatch in the side of the gondola.

TAKE-OFF

INTO THE STRATOSPHERE

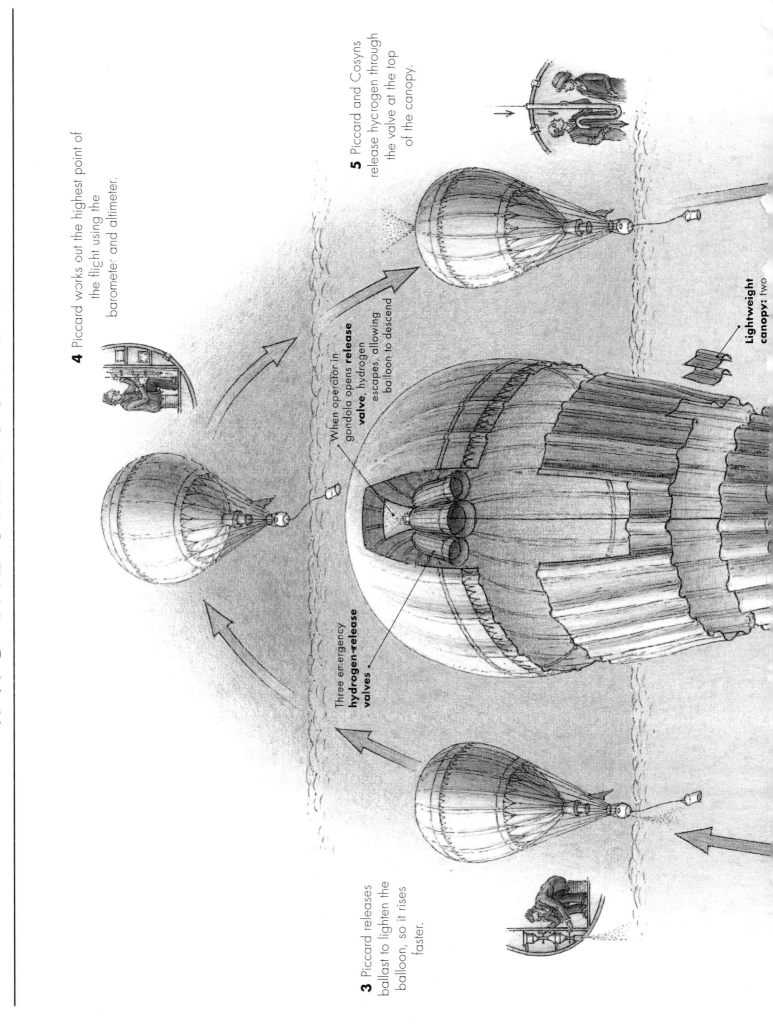

4 Piccard works out the highest point of the flight using the barometer and altimeter.

5 Piccard and Cosyns release hydrogen through the valve at the top of the canopy.

When operator in gondola opens **release valve**, hydrogen escapes, allowing balloon to descend

Three emergency **hydrogen-release valves**

3 Piccard releases ballast to lighten the balloon, so it rises faster.

Lightweight canopy: two

INSIDE THE GONDOLA

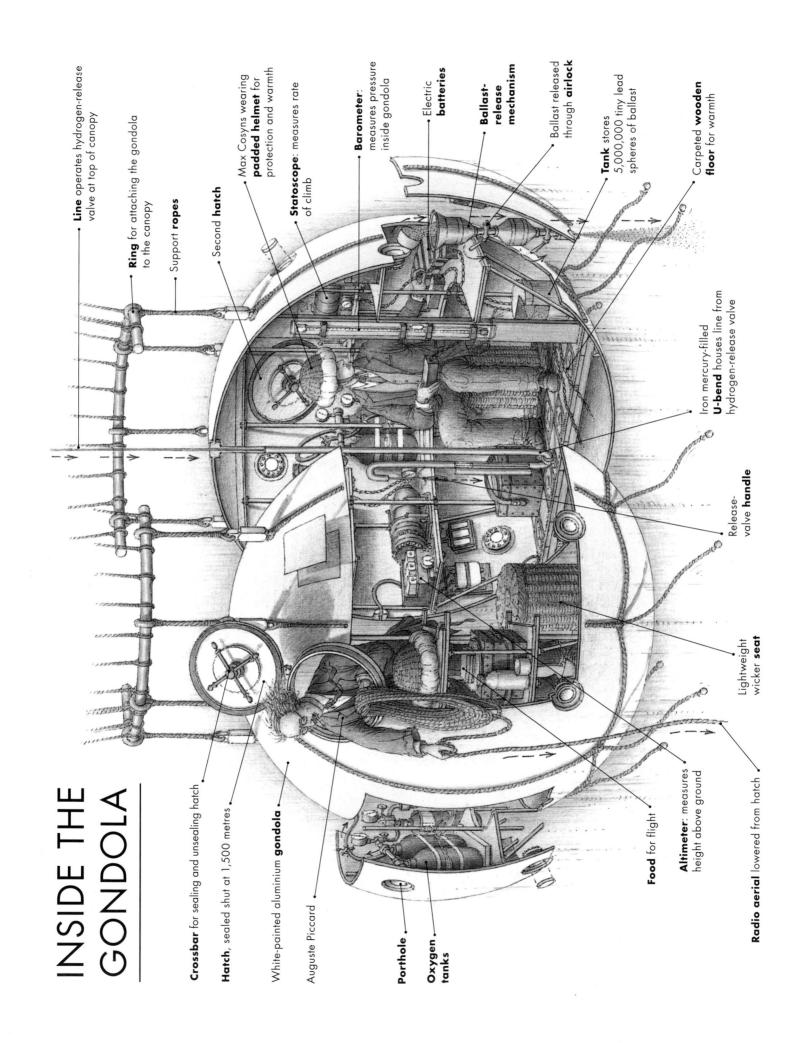

Crossbar for sealing and unsealing hatch

Hatch, sealed shut at 1,500 metres

White-painted aluminium **gondola**

Auguste Piccard

Porthole

Oxygen tanks

Food for flight

Altimeter: measures height above ground

Radio aerial lowered from hatch

Line operates hydrogen-release valve at top of canopy

Ring for attaching the gondola to the canopy

Support **ropes**

Second **hatch**

Max Cosyns wearing **padded helmet** for protection and warmth

Statoscope: measures rate of climb

Barometer: measures pressure inside gondola

Electric **batteries**

Ballast-release mechanism

Ballast released through **airlock**

Tank stores 5,000,000 tiny lead spheres of ballast

Carpeted **wooden floor** for warmth

Iron mercury-filled **U-bend** houses line from hydrogen-release valve

Release-valve **handle**

Lightweight wicker **seat**

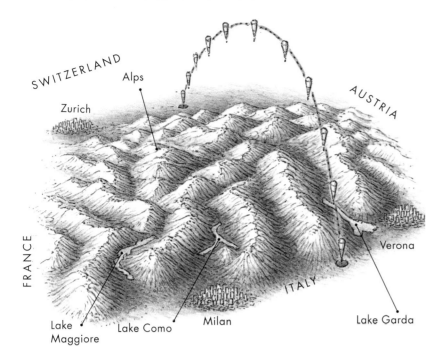

The path of Auguste Piccard's second flight into the stratosphere.

The following year, the *FNRS* flew again. This time Auguste was accompanied by a Belgian engineer, Professor Max Cosyns. On 18 August, they took off from Dübendorf Aerodrome near Zurich, drifted high above southern Switzerland and northern Italy, crossed Lake Garda and landed near the Italian resort of Desenzano. This time all went well, and they were able to make the scientific observations they needed. What's more, they beat their own record, reaching an amazing 16,200 metres.

A further 25 ascents followed over the next few years. Piccard pushed the world altitude record to 23,000 metres and gathered vital information about the stratosphere and those strange cosmic rays. As it turned out, they were not rays at all, but minute space invaders: sub-atomic particles zooming into Earth's atmosphere from elsewhere in the universe. He saw no angels, either.

By the time of his last balloon adventure, Auguste Piccard knew that the principles of his

pressurized cabin could also take him to the depths of the ocean. Working with his son, Jacques, he began to design an extraordinary deep-sea craft, or bathyscaphe. They named it the *Trieste*.

Instead of a balloon canopy, the *Trieste* had a long cylinder-shaped float. Inside the float were a large petrol tank and two air tanks. Petrol and air are lighter than water so, when all three tanks were full, the craft remained on the surface. To make it sink, the air tanks were flooded with sea water. The float also contained two hoppers filled with iron pellets to release when the bathyscaphe needed to rise again.

An air-tight cabin was welded beneath the float. Like the cabin of the *FNRS*, it was a perfect sphere, but instead of aluminium, its walls were forged in steel 12.7 centimetres thick. It had two windows, made of a strong artificial glass called Lucite. And it had an air supply and purification system that allowed two crew members to

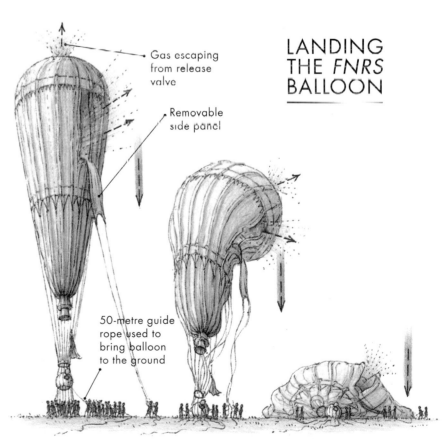

LANDING THE *FNRS* BALLOON

Gas escaping from release valve

Removable side panel

50-metre guide rope used to bring balloon to the ground

1 Valve at top and panel at side opened to release hydrogen gas

2 Balloon quickly deflates

3 Collapsed balloon

breathe safely for up to 24 hours.

Built in Italy, the *Trieste* was bought by the US Navy in 1958. The following year, the freighter *Santa Maria* transported it west from California to Guam. The USS *Wandank* then towed it a further 320 kilometres to a site above the deepest part of all the world's seas: the mysterious Challenger Deep. This great gash in the earth's surface, deeper than Mount Everest is high, lies in the Mariana Trench on the floor of the Pacific Ocean.

Here, in rough seas, Jacques Piccard and Lieutenant Don Walsh of the US Navy undertook one of the most nerve-jangling journeys ever made. On the morning of 23 January 1960, the two men climbed through the hatch and sealed themselves into their steel bubble. At 8.23 a.m. precisely, they let sea water into the air tanks above them and began a 288-minute descent, down, down to the funeral-black floor of the ocean.

To Jacques' surprise and dismay, at just over 100 metres below the surface, the *Trieste* came to a stop. It had met a dense layer of cold water (a thermocline), which blocked their descent. After a quick calculation, he made his craft less buoyant by releasing some of the petrol from the tank above, and the *Trieste* continued dropping into the darkness.

At 300 metres, Jacques tested the *Trieste*'s quartz arclights, casting bright white beams into the surrounding sea. Plankton streamed past. By 730 metres they had moved from the "twilight zone" to the "abyssal zone", where not a trace of sunlight can reach. Staring out at the grim blackness, the men felt the cabin grow colder and colder.

Around 5,500 metres, the cabin sprang a small leak, which a little later mended itself. Now dropping at 61 metres a minute, the *Trieste* plummeted beyond 7,000 metres, reaching a new record depth for any dive. At 9,000 metres, Jacques could feel the steep walls of the Mariana Trench rising around them.

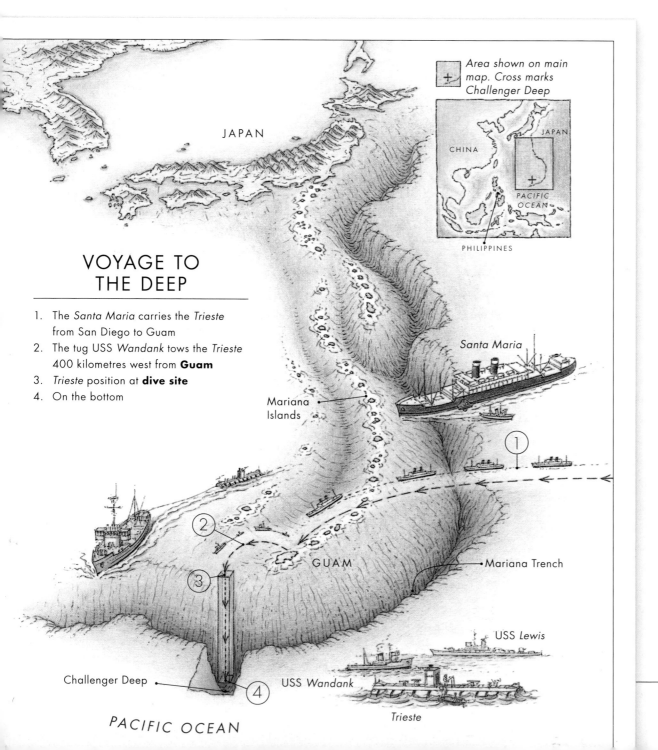

VOYAGE TO THE DEEP

1. The *Santa Maria* carries the *Trieste* from San Diego to Guam
2. The tug USS *Wandank* tows the *Trieste* 400 kilometres west from **Guam**
3. *Trieste* position at **dive site**
4. On the bottom

Area shown on main map. Cross marks Challenger Deep

CHINA
JAPAN
PACIFIC OCEAN
PHILIPPINES

JAPAN

Mariana Islands

Santa Maria

GUAM

Mariana Trench

Challenger Deep

USS *Wandank*

USS *Lewis*

Trieste

PACIFIC OCEAN

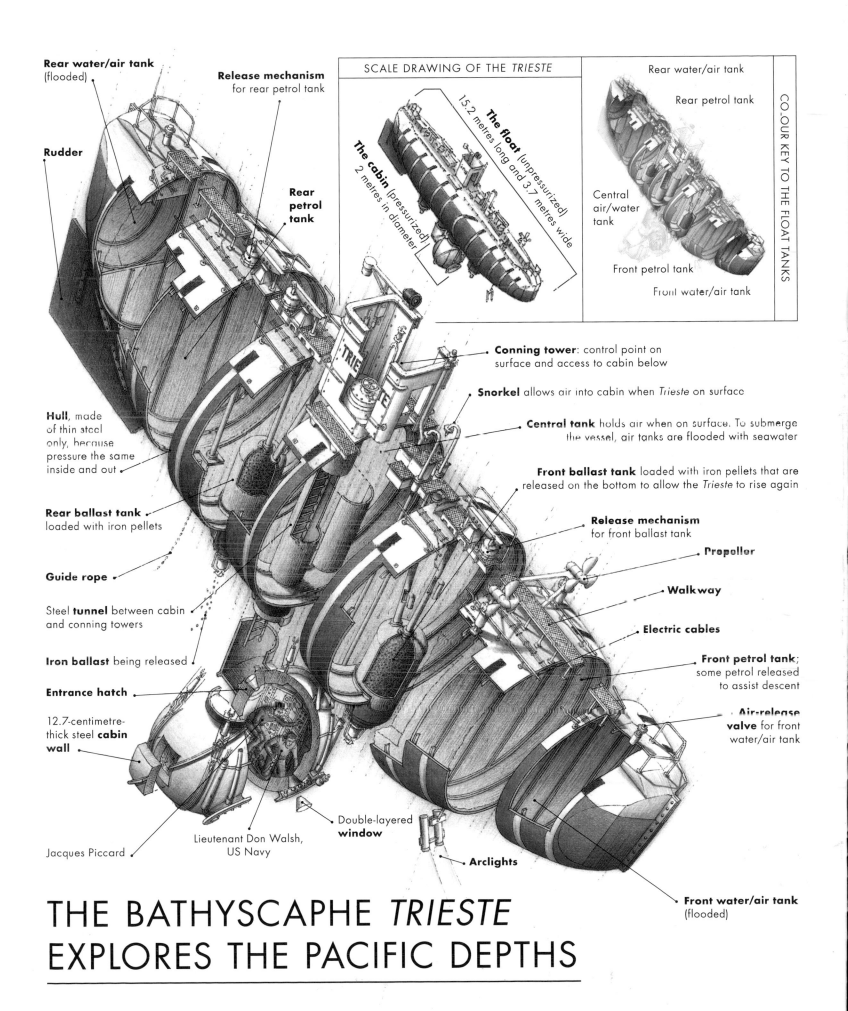

Rear water/air tank (flooded)

Release mechanism for rear petrol tank

Rudder

Rear petrol tank

Hull, made of thin steel only, because pressure the same inside and out

Rear ballast tank loaded with iron pellets

Guide rope

Steel **tunnel** between cabin and conning towers

Iron ballast being released

Entrance hatch

12.7-centimetre-thick steel **cabin wall**

Jacques Piccard

Lieutenant Don Walsh, US Navy

Double-layered **window**

Arclights

SCALE DRAWING OF THE *TRIESTE*

The float (unpressurized) 15.2 metres long and 3.7 metres wide

The cabin (pressurized) 2 metres in diameter

Rear water/air tank

Rear petrol tank

Central air/water tank

Front petrol tank

Front water/air tank

COLOUR KEY TO THE FLOAT TANKS

Conning tower: control point on surface and access to cabin below

Snorkel allows air into cabin when *Trieste* on surface

Central tank holds air when on surface. To submerge the vessel, air tanks are flooded with seawater

Front ballast tank loaded with iron pellets that are released on the bottom to allow the *Trieste* to rise again

Release mechanism for front ballast tank

Propeller

Walkway

Electric cables

Front petrol tank; some petrol released to assist descent

Air-release valve for front water/air tank

Front water/air tank (flooded)

THE BATHYSCAPHE *TRIESTE* EXPLORES THE PACIFIC DEPTHS

200,000 tonnes (1.124 tonnes per square centimetre), equivalent to the weight of five A380 Airbuses

Depth measured
in Empire State
Buildings:
443 metres each

USS Lewis

Continental shelf

USS Wandank

Arclight shining

Releasing
petrol

At sea level
Trieste's air tanks
are flooded with
seawater and she
begins to sink

**100 metres
below**
Piccard releases
petrol to allow
Trieste to descend
through a
cold layer

300 metres
Arclights
switched on

600 metres
Speed of descent
now increases from
10 centimetres
per second to 90
centimetres per
second

730 metres

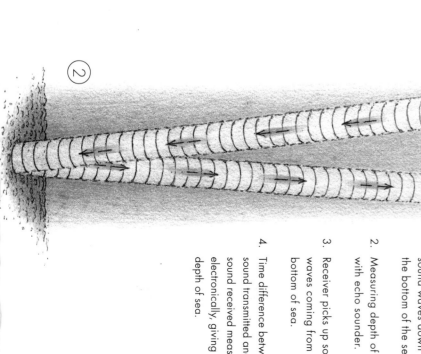

KEY

Piccard and Walsh
recorded the depth
of water under
the Trieste with an
electrical device
called an echo
sounder.

1. Transmitter sending
sound waves down to
the bottom of the sea.

2. Measuring depth of sea
with echo sounder.

3. Receiver picks up sound
waves coming from
bottom of sea.

4. Time difference between
sound transmitted and
sound received measured
electronically, giving
depth of sea.

Abyssal plain: level of the Pacific Ocean floor

here on down

5,500 metres
Cabin springs a leak but seals itself

7,000 metres
Trieste sets a new record for the deepest ever dive

8,300 metres
Piccard dumps some ballast to slow the rate of descent

9,100 metres
Alarm as outer windowpane cracks

9,500 metres
Piccard uses echo sounder to detect bottom of trench

10,900 metres
Trieste comes to rest on the bottom of the Challenger Deep

The *Trieste* had not been tested to this depth and he released some iron ballast to slow her speed. The ocean floor was still more than a kilometre away.

Suddenly, the men were shaken by what sounded like a muffled explosion. The outer skin of one of the windows had cracked. For a second, they thought they were finished. Luckily the inner layer of Lucite held fast, and not long afterwards the *Trieste* came to rest at the bottom of the Challenger Deep. Switching on their lights again, they stared out in wonder at the fish and slime around them. It was certainly eerie and strange – but at least there were no monsters.

As it would be dangerous to surface at night, the *Trieste* could not stay long. After just 20 minutes, Piccard lightened his craft by releasing nine tonnes of iron pellets from the hoppers in the float. The *Trieste* immediately began to rise. Faster and faster she climbed, until she was moving upwards at 1.5 metres per second. Just over three hours later, she broke the surface of the warm, bright Pacific. The sailors on the *Wandank*, and the escorting destroyer *Lewis*, hurried to winch her from the water and release her crew.

Since that famous January day, no human being has ever again dared venture into the Challenger Deep. The amazing Piccards are still the only explorers to have travelled literally to both the heights and the depths of our world. ✪

ON THE ROOF OF THE WORLD

Tenzing Norgay and Edmund Hillary scale Mount Everest, 1953

While Auguste Piccard was flying to the stratosphere in a balloon, other explorers were trying to reach almost as high on foot. One of their main goals was a mighty summit that soars into the clear, unpolluted air of the Himalayan mountains. Europeans called it first Peak XV, and later Everest after the British surveyor who had overseen the work of measuring it. But the Tibetans have always known it as Chomolungma, or Goddess Mother of the World. The name could not be more apt, for this great Goddess Mother is the highest point on the earth's surface.

Although the mountain's height was first known in 1856, almost another century passed before anyone scaled it. There were plenty of attempts, though. Between 1921 and 1952, eight major expeditions set out to reach the top. None succeeded, and some did not return, but each attempt contributed to a growing sum of knowledge about the mountain.

The weather in the high Himalayas is terrible. All winter, north-west winds blow at speeds of up to 160 kilometres per hour, making it impossible even to stand. Temperatures seldom rise above -30°C. In summer, the monsoon brings months of heavy snow. Over time, however, climbers learned of two short lulls between these treacherous seasons, one in late May and the other in early October.

Mountaineers also faced the problem of thin air. As the first balloonists and aviators discovered, the amount of oxygen in the atmosphere decreases rapidly the higher you go. The effects are drastic. At 3,000 metres, the brain loses 10 per cent of the oxygen it needs for thinking. At 5,500 metres, 50 per cent is lost and moving becomes difficult. Above 8,000 metres, 70 per cent is lost and it is hard to sleep, drink or eat. Yet Everest stands a towering 8,850 metres above sea level. No one knew for sure whether it was even possible to survive that high.

Trip by trip, climbers learned that their bodies could adapt to fairly high altitude, if they had time to acclimatize. For heights over 6,000 metres, they tried using bottled oxygen, developed for aircraft crew. The masks were uncomfortable and the bottles heavy, but breathing with oxygen greatly improved their strength and concentration.

Another difficulty was how to find a route through Everest's shifting glaciers, gaping crevasses and deadly avalanche zones. Slowly, explorers pieced together a picture of the mountain's terrain. By the early 1950s, helped by World War II aerial photographs, they had found what looked like a possible way to the summit.

In 1952, a Swiss expedition approached the mountain from the south. First they climbed up a gigantic cascade of shifting ice, 610 metres high. This is the terrifying Khumbu Icefall. At its top, they crossed a beautiful hidden valley that earlier expeditions had named the Western Cwm. Its floor is smooth ice. At the other end of the Cwm, they climbed a 1,200-metre snow wall on the side of Everest's neighbour, Lhotse, to reach the South Col. This is a windy pass of ice and rock lying only 850 metres from the peak. From here the Swiss climbed to the South-east Ridge to reach a record height of 8,600 metres before being forced back by bad weather and faulty oxygen sets.

The following spring, a British expedition led by John Hunt tried again. Hunt was an experienced soldier who knew the vital importance of preparation and planning. To allow for sickness and injury, he chose a large team of ten climbers, including two New Zealanders, George Lowe and Edmund Hillary. When they reached Nepal, the men would be joined by a group of experienced Sherpas, led by Tenzing Norgay.

The party chose and tested their equipment carefully. Modern materials helped them. Strong light nylon windproofed the climbers' padded clothing. Their boots were soled with flexible rubber rather than traditional leather, and lightweight aluminium was used for the frames of their backpacks and for the expedition's ladder.

Hunt understood the importance of diet, too. Griffith Pugh, one of the expedition doctors, calculated the number of calories each climber would need on the mountain, and made up army-style ration packs. At lower and middle altitudes, he knew, the men would have enormous appetites. At great heights, where their bodies needed food and liquid most, they would hardly want to eat or drink at all. In such circumstances, high-energy sugar, jam, biscuits and sweets were best, washed down with hot drinks of soup, cocoa and lemonade.

Hunt planned to pitch a series of camps up the mountain, perhaps as many as eight. Each would be well stocked with food, fuel, sleeping bags, oxygen and climbing gear. From the highest, he hoped to send out two or possibly three assault parties at the end of May. If the climbers were fit and the weather good, he hoped that one of these might reach the summit.

On 10 March 1953, the expedition set out from Kathmandu, the capital city of Nepal. As there were no roads into the mountains, a team of 350 local porters divided up the 7.5 tonnes of equipment and carried it on their backs. At this point, the climbers were also joined

At extreme altitude, the mountaineers found they could sleep better when wearing oxygen masks.

by the skilled Sherpa hillmen, whose job was to assist them with the tough work on the mountain.

The march east through the hills took 17 days. For the climbers, it was a chance to adapt to their new surroundings and to get to know each other and the Sherpas better. They passed through spectacular scenery, occasionally catching glimpses of Everest in the distance.

At first, the track wound through lush fields and woods, where wild rhododendron and magnolia grew. On the ninth day, the track rose into the Sola Khumbu district, home of the Sherpa people. Here the country was more rugged, the air cooler. The main village, Namche Bazar, which they reached on 25 March, stands at 3,480 metres above sea level. Everest's bleak face was now beginning to loom closer.

The next stage of the climb brought them to the Buddhist monastery of Thyangboche, which sits in green meadows at around 4,000 metres. Here the porters were paid and set off home. With the monks' permission, the rest of the party pitched camp and spent three weeks training, acclimatizing and testing their oxygen equipment.

Finally, in mid-April, the whole expedition moved up the valley to establish base camp at the foot of the Khumbu Icefall. From there the mountaineers began the exhausting task of manhandling tents, food and equipment, step by difficult step, up the mountainside.

The work took several weeks. At times, bad weather and illness almost brought it to a halt. But by 24 May, Camp 8 was established on the South Col, from where Hunt decided to make two attempts on the summit. He had already picked his teams. Tom Bourdillon and Charles Evans would go first, followed by Edmund Hillary and Tenzing Norgay.

Bourdillon and Evans set out on the morning of 26 May. Using closed-circuit oxygen sets, they made good progress. Before long they had climbed higher than the Swiss had reached, higher than anyone had ever been before. But on gaining the South Summit, they made an unexpected discovery. Everest's true peak, which they were the first to see, lay at the top of one further ridge. They knew that they did not have enough time or oxygen to climb that far and return to Camp 8 before dark. Rather than risk almost certain death, the disappointed men turned back.

Norgay and Hillary set out two days later, on 28 May. Learning from the others, they brought a tent with them. That night they established Camp 9, just below the South Summit. It was so cold that Hillary's boots froze solid. Next morning he had to cook them over the stove before he could get them on. After a breakfast of sardines on biscuits, washed down with lemon juice sweetened with sugar, the pair set out for the South Summit at 6.30 a.m. From there, they would try their luck on the untested final ridge.

Five gruelling hours later, the two men found themselves gazing over the grandest view on Earth. Hillary looked at his watch: 11.30 a.m., Friday 29 May 1953. Delighted and relieved, they took off their oxygen sets and thumped and hugged each other. Norgay buried food offerings for the mountain's gods. Hillary dropped a small cross in the snow and took photographs. After 15 minutes they turned to go. If they were careful, they had just enough time and oxygen to reach Camp 8 before nightfall. Below that, safety, comfort and worldwide fame awaited them. ✪

A MOUNTAINEER'S CLOTHING & EQUIPMENT FOR OVER 6,000 METRES

Snow **goggles**
Breathing **mask**
Nylon **outer hood**
Goose-down **hood**
String **vest**
Open-circuit **oxygen set**
Goose-down **sleeping bag**
Air **mattress**
Spare **clothes**
Nylon **outer jacket**
Goose-down **jacket**
One thick wool **jersey**
Two thin wool jerseys
Woollen **shirt**
Silk **glove**
Woollen **mitten**
Nylon **outer gauntlet**
Woollen **underpants**
Goose-down **trousers**
Nylon **outer trousers**
Goose-down **socks**
Three pairs of wool socks
Sprung metal **loop** (karabiner)
Metal **peg** (piton)
Ice axe
Boot
Crampons
Kapok layer, sandwiched between leather **uppers**
Rubber **sole**
Nylon **rope** attached to another climber

FROM KATHMANDU TO BASE CAMP

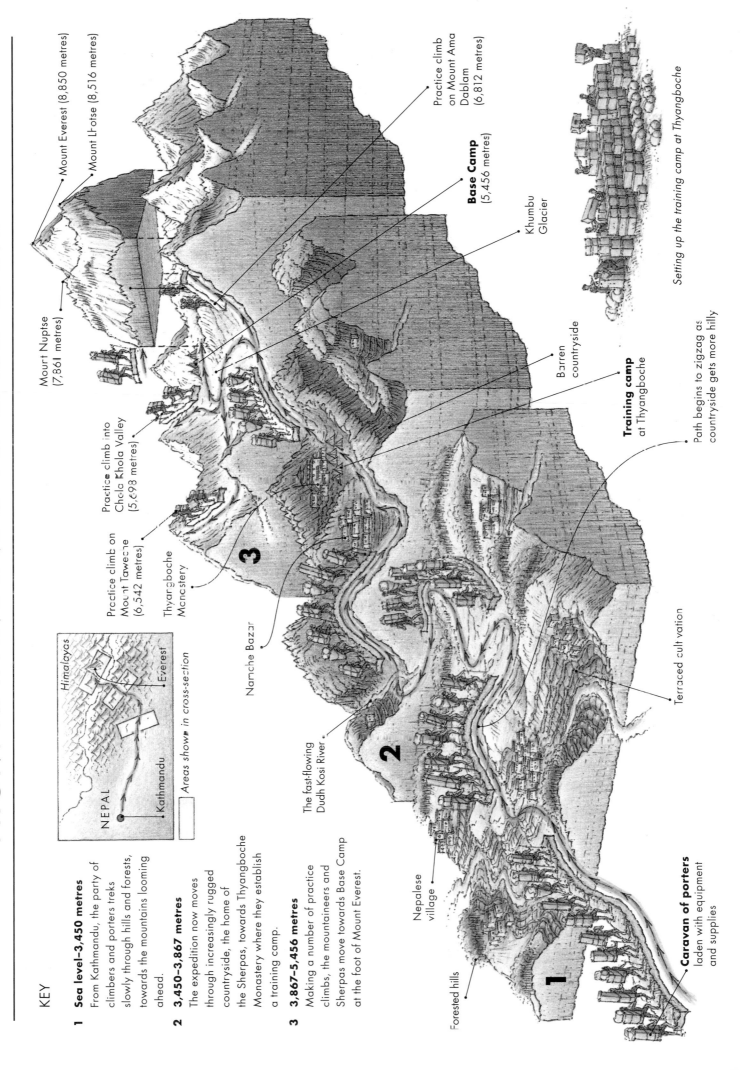

KEY

1 Sea level–3,450 metres
From Kathmandu, the party of climbers and porters treks slowly through hills and forests, towards the mountains looming ahead.

2 3,450–3,867 metres
The expedition now moves through increasingly rugged countryside, the home of the Sherpas, towards Thyangboche Monastery where they establish a training camp.

3 3,867–5,456 metres
Making a number of practice climbs, the mountaineers and Sherpas move towards Base Camp at the foot of Mount Everest.

Himalayas

NEPAL

Kathmandu

Everest

Areas shown in cross-section

Mount Everest (8,850 metres)

Mount Lhotse (8,516 metres)

Mount Nuptse (7,861 metres)

Practice climb on Mount Ama Dablam (6,812 metres)

Base Camp (5,456 metres)

Khumbu Glacier

Practice climb into Chola Khola Valley (5,693 metres)

Practice climb on Mount Taweche (6,542 metres)

Thyangboche Monastery

Nanche Bazar

Setting up the training camp at Thyangboche

Barren countryside

Training camp at Thyangboche

Path begins to zigzag as countryside gets more hilly

The fast-flowing Dudh Kosi River

Terraced cultivation

Nepalese village

Forested hills

Caravan of porters laden with equipment and supplies

THE FINAL ASSAULT

To avoid long and exhausting climbs at high altitude, Hunt's party moved up Everest in carefully organized steps. Each one began and ended from a well-stocked base where climbers could relax and recover. This meant that the final and most dangerous climb to the summit was made over a comparatively short distance.

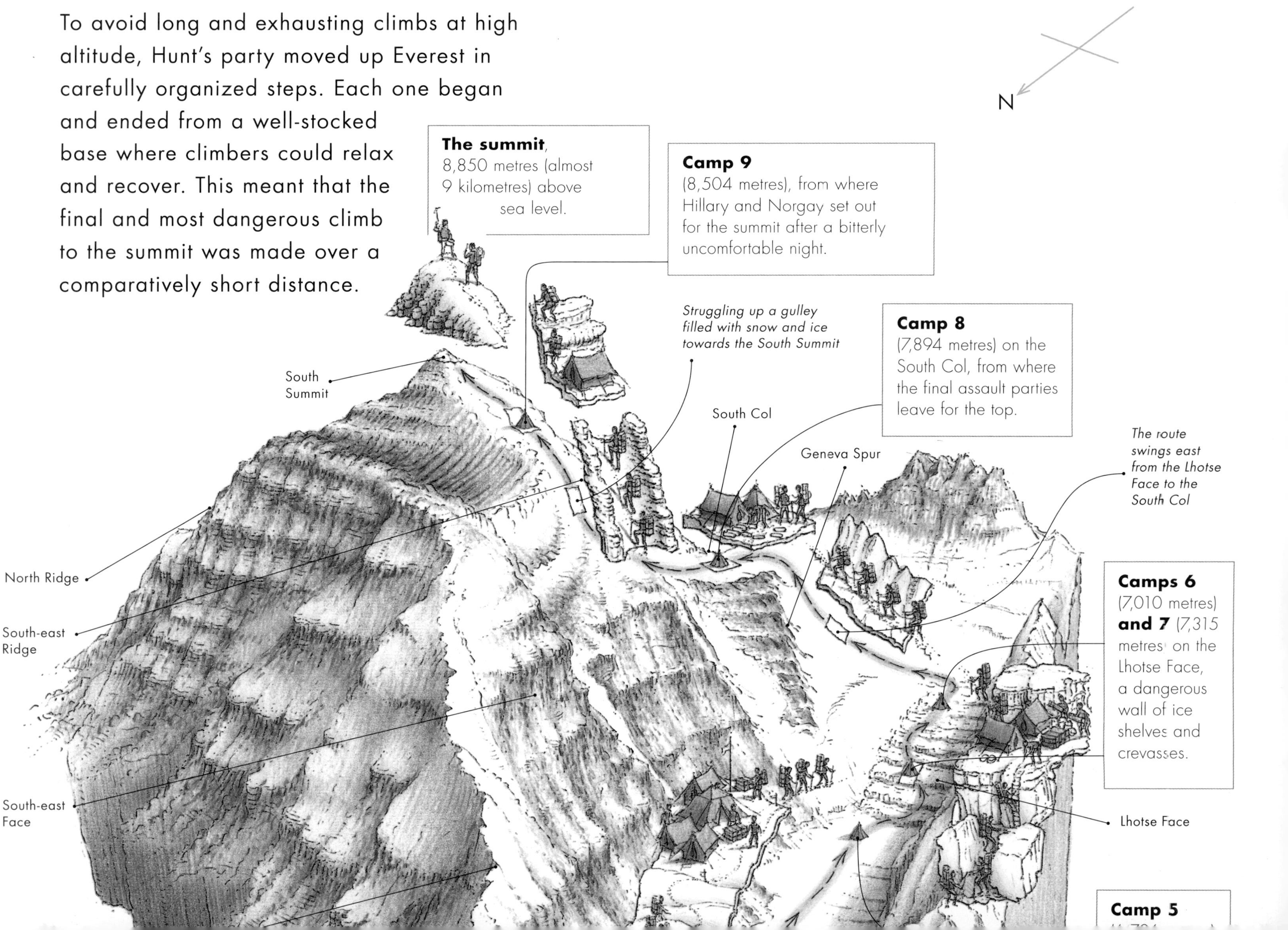

N

The summit
8,850 metres (almost 9 kilometres) above sea level.

Camp 9
(8,504 metres), from where Hillary and Norgay set out for the summit after a bitterly uncomfortable night.

Camp 8
(7,894 metres) on the South Col, from where the final assault parties leave for the top.

Struggling up a gulley filled with snow and ice towards the South Summit

The route swings east from the Lhotse Face to the South Col

Camps 6 (7,010 metres) **and 7** (7,315 metres) on the Lhotse Face, a dangerous wall of ice shelves and crevasses.

Lhotse Face

Camp 5

Geneva Spur

South Col

South Summit

North Ridge

South-east Ridge

South-east Face

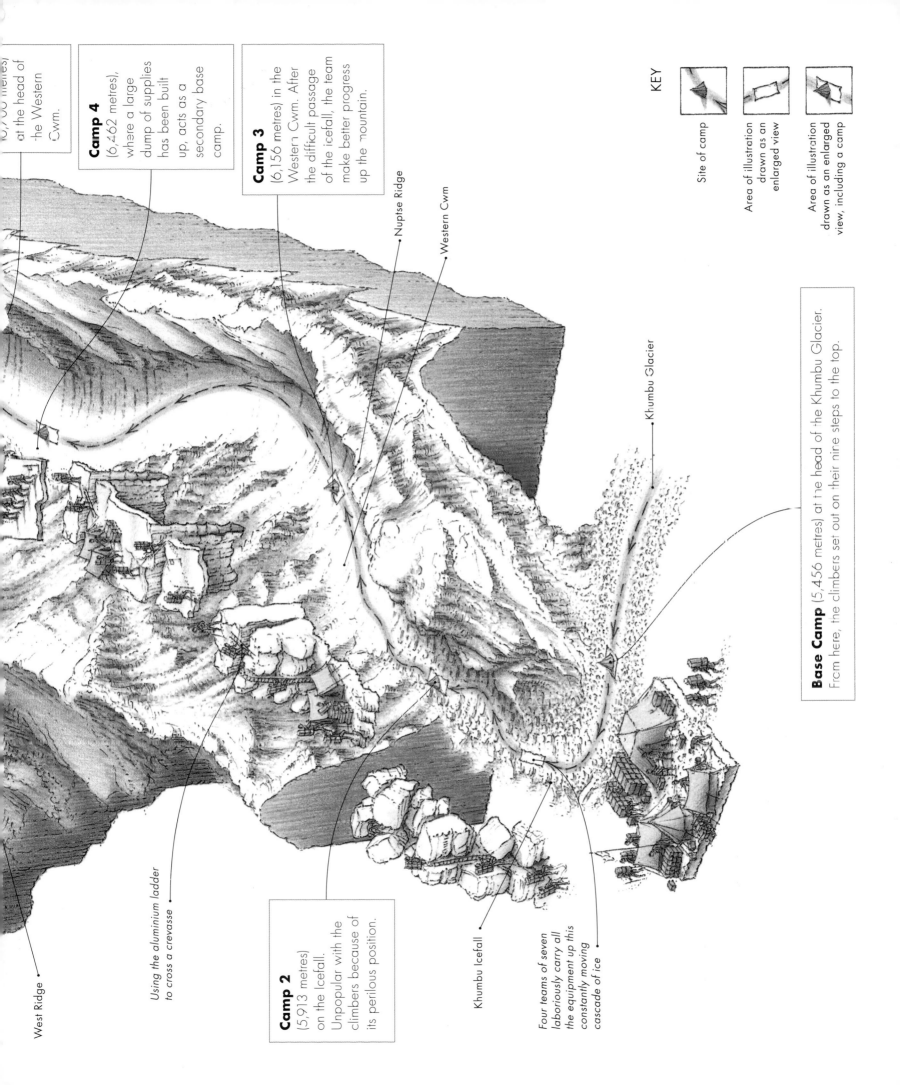

...(6,700 metres) at the head of the Western Cwm.

Camp 4

(6,462 metres), where a large dump of supplies has been built up, acts as a secondary base camp.

Camp 3

(6,156 metres) in the Western Cwm. After the difficult passage of the icefall, the team make better progress up the mountain.

Nuptse Ridge

Western Cwm

Camp 2

(5,913 metres) on the Icefall. Unpopular with the climbers because of its perilous position.

Using the aluminium ladder to cross a crevasse

West Ridge

Khumbu Icefall

Four teams of seven laboriously carry all the equipment up this constantly moving cascade of ice

Khumbu Glacier

Base Camp (5,456 metres) at the head of the Khumbu Glacier. From here, the climbers set out on their nine steps to the top.

KEY

Site of camp

Area of illustration drawn as an enlarged view

Area of illustration drawn as an enlarged view, including a camp

MAN ON THE MOON

Apollo 11 rockets into space, 1969

Since the beginning of history, it has been worshipped as a god and as a goddess... Tides are pulled by it, calendars counted by it, travellers journey by it and artists are inspired by it... It is our nearest neighbour, our glorious silvery night light – the moon.

At 384,000 kilometres from Earth, the moon is 400 times closer to us than the sun, and 100 times closer than Venus. On a clear night, it is possible to see its surface clearly. But not until the end of the nineteenth century did anyone seriously consider landing on it.

While balloonists and aviators were exploring the skies, others were thinking about ways to travel even higher, into space itself. The challenges were huge. To lift itself off the ground and rise 100 kilometres into orbit, a craft has to reach speeds of around 27,350 kilometres per hour; to break free from Earth's gravity and enter deep space, it then has to accelerate to a staggering 45,000 kilometres per hour. Such speeds require hugely powerful engines, burning vast quantities of liquid fuel – fuel that is itself heavy, needing even larger engines to lift it, and so on...

In the early twentieth century, independent scientists working in Russia, America and Germany discovered the basic principles of rocket propulsion. In the 1940s, a German engineer, Wernher von Braun, pulled their ideas together to build the V-2 rocket, which flew faster, higher and further than any previous machine ever made. The Nazi government used the V-2 as a deadly missile in World War II, but von Braun dreamed of using his rockets for space exploration.

After the war, von Braun settled in North America, designing rockets for the US army. Meanwhile, thousands of miles away inside the Soviet Union (Russia), other scientists were making rockets of their own. In 1957, they sparked a "space race" between the two nations when they launched the first ever man-made satellite, *Sputnik 1*, into orbit round the earth. A month later, the Soviets launched a dog, Laika, into Earth orbit in the spacecraft *Sputnik 2*. Alarmed, the Americans decided to boost spending on their own space programme. In 1958, they set up a specialist research agency, NASA (National Aeronautics and Space Administration), dedicated to space exploration. Wernher von Braun became one of its directors.

The Soviets stayed in the lead, however, and in April 1961, Yuri Gagarin became the first "spaceman", making a single orbit of Earth in 108 minutes in the spacecraft *Vostok 1*. A month later the newly elected American president, John F. Kennedy, responded by raising the stakes. On 21 May, he declared, *"I believe that this nation should commit itself to achieving the goal, before this decade is out, of landing a man on the moon, and returning him safely to the earth."*

Talk about landing a man on the moon was one thing; actually doing it was another. Space is a harsh environment. With no oxygen or water, it is unsuitable for life. Moreover, beyond the pull of the earth's gravity, objects float free, making the simplest actions difficult to perform. In space, for instance, nothing

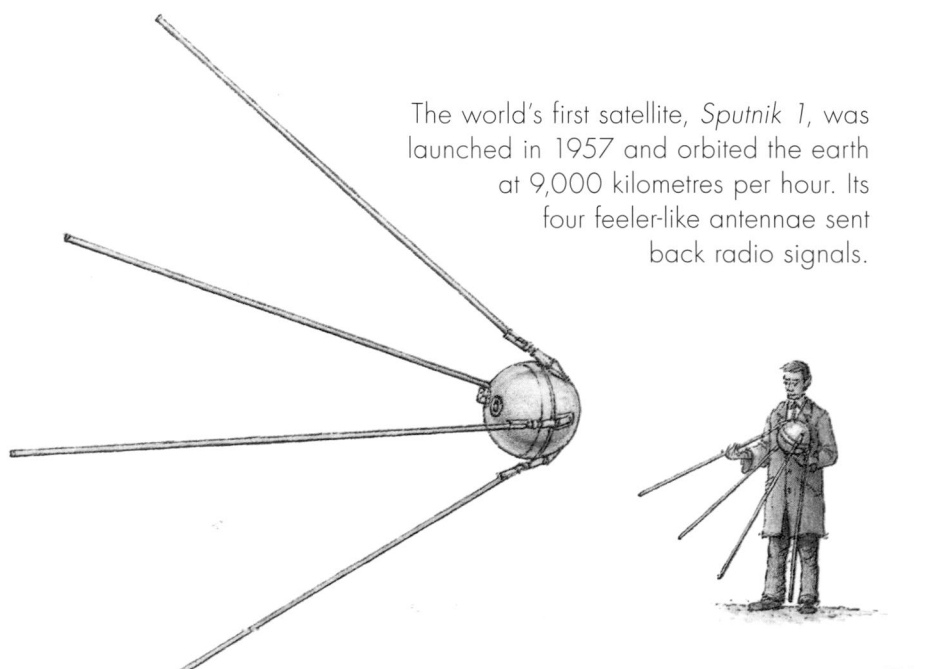

The world's first satellite, *Sputnik 1*, was launched in 1957 and orbited the earth at 9,000 kilometres per hour. Its four feeler-like antennae sent back radio signals.

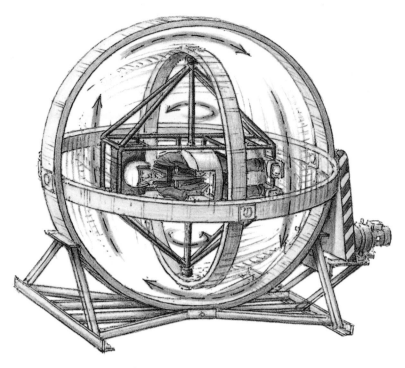

NASA's unpopular centrifuge machine whirled astronauts around to prepare them for the rigours of space travel.

comes out when you tip up a cup of liquid, and all drinking has to be done through a straw.

Bringing humans safely back from the moon is as dangerous as getting them there. Most rapidly moving objects approaching the earth from space are burned up by the friction created when they reach the atmosphere. This is what a shooting star is – a meteor burning up as it passes into our oxygen-rich atmosphere. While the problem was inconvenient for satellites or unmanned rockets, for manned craft it was – literally – a matter of life and death.

Finally, there was the question of how to make the journey. After much thought, von Braun and the NASA team decided it would be impossible to build a single spacecraft capable of landing on the moon's surface and returning to Earth. They chose instead to put a spacecraft in orbit round the moon, going down to the surface and back in a detachable "module".

Over the next few years, NASA sent pairs of astronauts on a series of test flights. These *Gemini* missions discovered how to link up and dock with another craft in space. They proved it was possible to survive in space for as long as two weeks, and to perform space walks of up to five and

a half hours outside their vehicle. They also carried the first computer into space, a piece of equipment that would be crucial for a moon mission.

Meanwhile, NASA was preparing a series of three-man flights. Codenamed "Project Apollo", it would try to land men on the moon. As it had to carry three astronauts, the *Apollo* spacecraft needed to be larger than the *Gemini* one. It was built in three sections. The cone-shaped Command Module was the control centre for the flight and the astronauts' living area. The Service Module housed a small rocket engine and carried the crew's oxygen supply, as well as food and water for three weeks. The third section was the Lunar Module, the small spaceship designed to carry two men down to the moon's surface, then bring them back again to the Command Module which was still in lunar orbit.

To launch the *Apollo* spacecraft, von Braun and his team designed and built one of the most remarkable machines ever made. The awe-inspiring *Saturn V* rocket was 110.6 metres tall and as broad as a motorway. To lift its 3,000 tonnes off the ground, five roaring rocket engines were packed together at the bottom. When these fired for take-off, flames swirled across

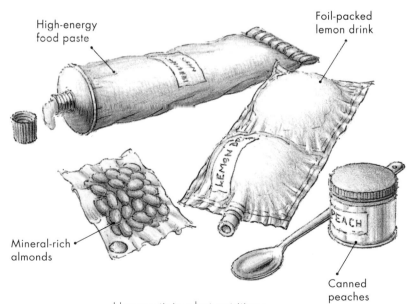

High-energy food paste

Foil-packed lemon drink

Mineral-rich almonds

Canned peaches

Unappetizing but nutritious, the astronauts' food was vacuum-packed and freeze-dried.

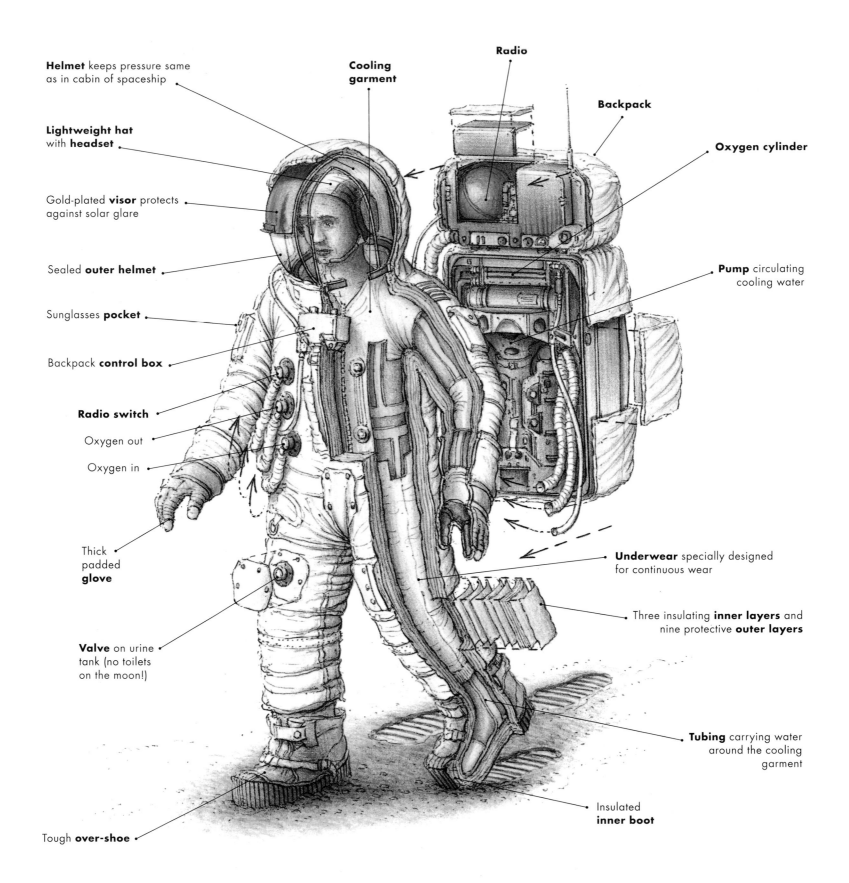

Helmet keeps pressure same as in cabin of spaceship

Lightweight hat with **headset**

Gold-plated **visor** protects against solar glare

Sealed **outer helmet**

Sunglasses **pocket**

Backpack **control box**

Radio switch

Oxygen out

Oxygen in

Thick padded **glove**

Valve on urine tank (no toilets on the moon!)

Tough **over-shoe**

Cooling garment

Radio

Backpack

Oxygen cylinder

Pump circulating cooling water

Underwear specially designed for continuous wear

Three insulating **inner layers** and nine protective **outer layers**

Tubing carrying water around the cooling garment

Insulated **inner boot**

WALKING ON THE MOON

The astronauts' spacesuits and life-support packs each weighed 86 kilograms on Earth, but just 14 kilograms on the moon.

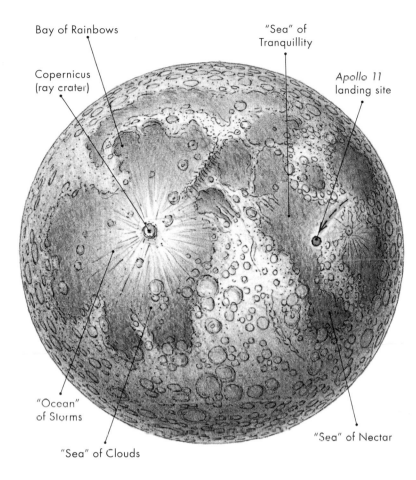

Bay of Rainbows

Copernicus (ray crater)

"Ocean" of Storms

"Sea" of Clouds

"Sea" of Tranquillity

Apollo 11 landing site

"Sea" of Nectar

The pockmarked surface of the moon: choosing a level landing place from NASA headquarters, 384,000 kilometres away, was a tricky business. Bringing a spaceship down to it was even trickier. The *Eagle* overshot its target by several kilometres.

the surrounding marshes and the ground shook 80 kilometres away. The Vehicle Assembly Building constructed to house it was, at the time, the biggest in the world. Standing 160 metres high, it had its own weather inside – including clouds.

To avoid carrying empty fuel tanks, *Saturn V* was built in three stages. Stage one powered it 61 kilometres above the launch pad, detached and fell back to Earth. Stage two burned for only a few minutes before it too fell away, and stage three took over. This put the spacecraft into Earth orbit, then fired again to send it on its way towards the moon.

The Apollo programme of manned and unmanned

launches began with earth orbital flights, then moved on to take a look at the moon itself. *Apollo 8* flew round behind the moon, giving its crew a sight of the dark side. *Apollo 10* sent a lunar module to within 15,200 metres of the moon's surface. So that the astronauts were not tempted to go any further, their module had not been fitted with its metal landing legs.

From the hundreds of candidates who came forward to train as astronauts, NASA selected just 23. Of those, only three were needed for the *Apollo 11* moon-landing mission. Late in 1968, Neil Armstrong was chosen to be overall Mission Commander, with Edwin "Buzz" Aldrin as Lunar Module pilot, and Michael Collins as Command Module pilot. All three men had flown on previous *Gemini* flights and proved themselves to be brave, reliable and experienced pilots.

Eventually, on 16 July 1969, *Apollo 11* was ready to fly. The mighty *Saturn V,* packed with fuel, sat on its launch pad at the John F. Kennedy Space Center, Florida. High on the nose, strapped down inside their Command Module, the crew waited anxiously. The roads and open spaces nearby were jammed with a million spectators. Around the world, many times that number watched on TV.

Countdown began. The engines ignited … five, four, three, two, one – lift-off! Thundering and roaring like an ancient Greek god, the great rocket rose into the warm morning air. After two minutes, 30 seconds, the first stage fell off and the second stage boosted the rocket to 24,600 kilometres per hour, before itself falling away. *Apollo 11* did a quick orbit of earth before speeding up again and shooting towards the moon.

By now, Armstrong, Aldrin and Collins were out of their seats and floating about their business in the pressurized Command Module (codenamed *Columbia*). One of their first tasks was to bring the Lunar Module (codenamed *Eagle*) out of its storage place above stage three and fix it on top of the Command Module. This left their spacecraft looking like a weird metal tree with fiery roots.

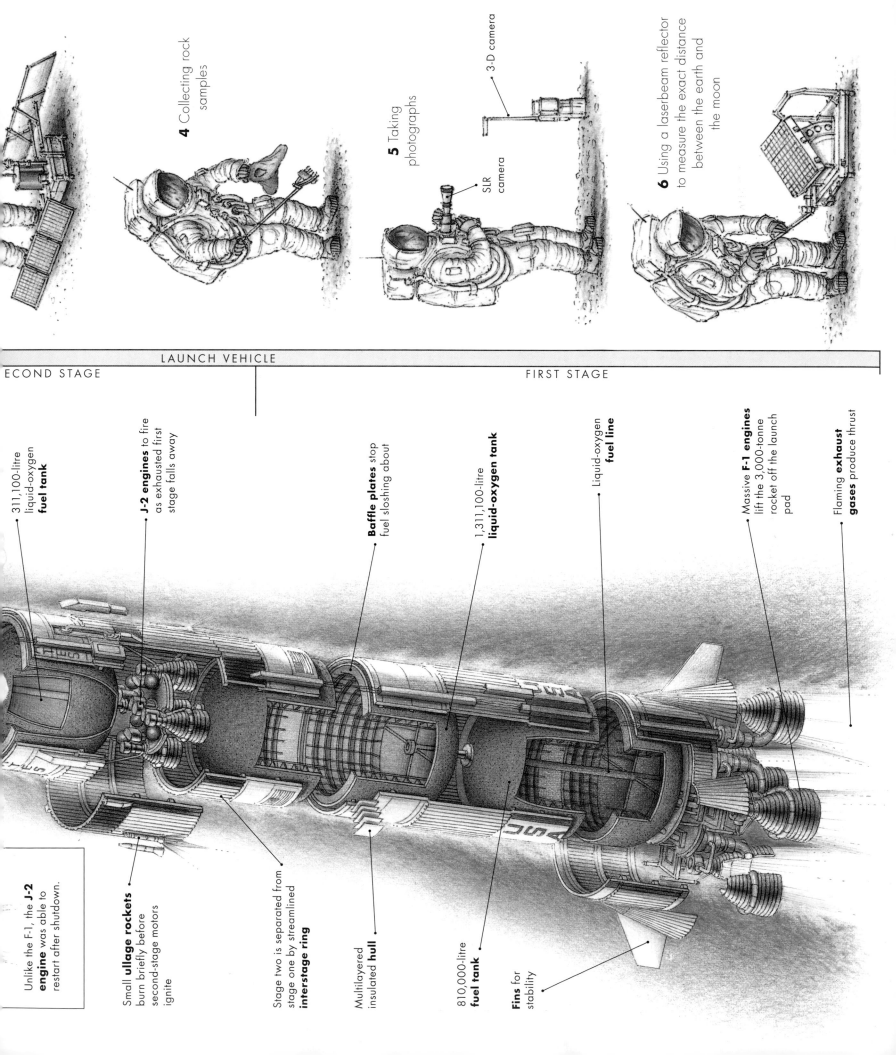

4 Collecting rock samples

5 Taking photographs

3-D camera

SLR camera

6 Using a laserbeam reflector to measure the exact distance between the earth and the moon

LAUNCH VEHICLE

ECOND STAGE

FIRST STAGE

311,100-litre liquid-oxygen **fuel tank**

J-2 engines to fire as exhausted first stage falls away

Baffle plates stop fuel sloshing about

1,311,100-litre **liquid-oxygen tank**

Liquid-oxygen **fuel line**

Massive **F-1 engines** lift the 3,000-tonne rocket off the launch pad

Flaming **exhaust gases** produce thrust

Unlike the F-1, the **J-2 engine** was able to restart after shutdown.

Small **ullage rockets** burn briefly before second-stage motors ignite

Stage two is separated from stage one by streamlined **interstage ring**

Multilayered insulated **hull**

810,000-litre **fuel tank**

Fins for stability

WORKING ON THE MOON

Some of the activities that Armstrong and Aldrin carried out while on the moon's surface.

1 Checking for lunar wind

2 Taking a core sample of the lunar surface

3 Measuring lunar seismic activity (movement beneath the surface)

APOLLO MODULES

THIRD STAGE

SATURN V BLAST-OFF!

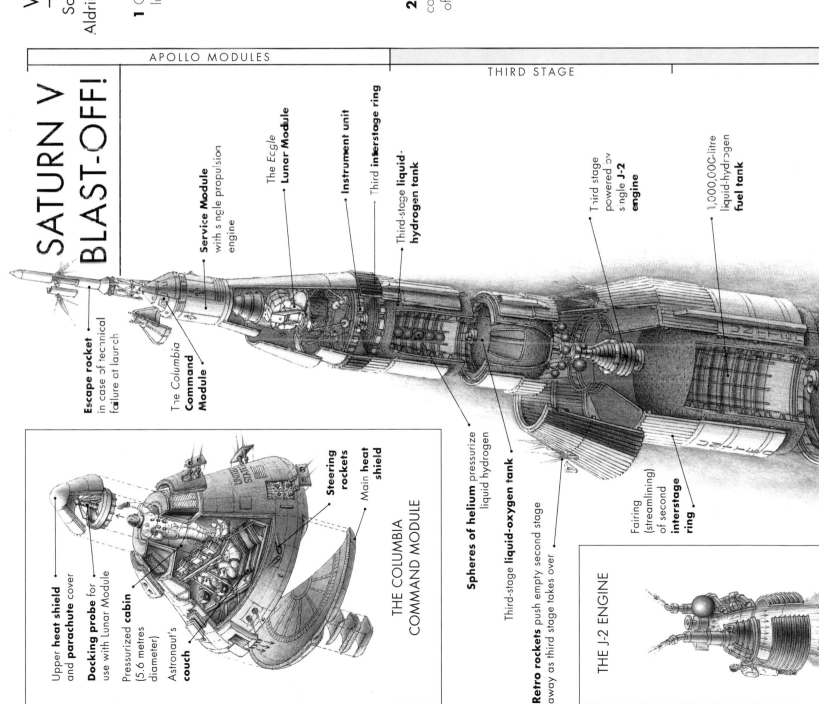

Escape rocket in case of technical failure at launch

The Columbia **Command Module**

Service Module with single propulsion engine

The *Eagle* **Lunar Module**

Instrument unit

Third **interstage ring**

Third-stage **liquid-hydrogen tank**

Third stage powered by single **J-2 engine**

1,000,000-litre liquid-hydrogen **fuel tank**

Spheres of helium pressurize liquid hydrogen

Third-stage **liquid-oxygen tank**

Retro rockets push empty second stage away as third stage takes over

Fairing (streamlining) of second **interstage ring**

THE COLUMBIA COMMAND MODULE

Upper **heat shield** and **parachute** cover

Docking probe for use with Lunar Module

Pressurized **cabin** (5.6 metres diameter)

Astronaut's **couch**

Steering rockets

Main **heat shield**

THE J-2 ENGINE

THE *EAGLE* LUNAR MODULE

The two-part spaceship that carried Aldrin and Armstrong from *Columbia* to the surface of the moon and back.

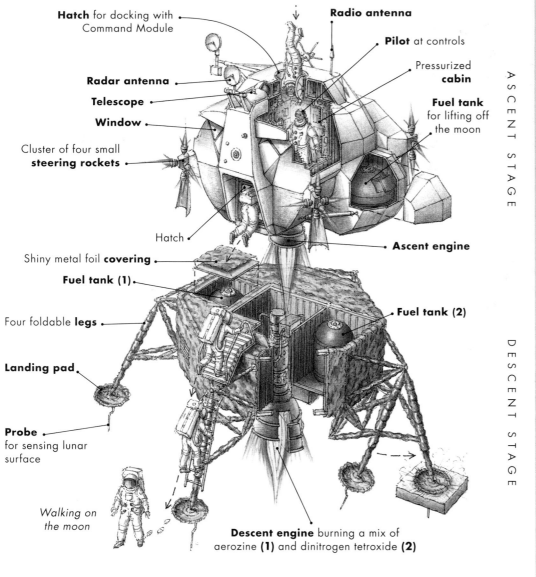

Hatch for docking with Command Module

Radar antenna

Telescope

Window

Cluster of four small **steering rockets**

Hatch

Shiny metal foil **covering**

Fuel tank (1)

Four foldable **legs**

Landing pad

Probe for sensing lunar surface

Walking on the moon

Radio antenna

Pilot at controls

Pressurized **cabin**

Fuel tank for lifting off the moon

Ascent engine

Fuel tank (2)

Descent engine burning a mix of aerozine **(1)** and dinitrogen tetroxide **(2)**

ASCENT STAGE

DESCENT STAGE

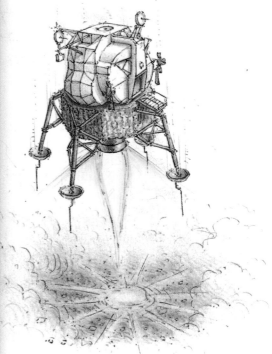

As the pilot could not see the ground directly beneath him, long thin landing probes were lowered from the *Eagle*'s pads to sense when the surface was close and the engine could be cut.

Three days later, *Apollo 11* went into orbit around the moon. Now came the really tricky bit, a manoeuvre never before attempted. Armstrong and Aldrin climbed out of the Command Module into the Lunar Module, and sealed the hatch. While Collins continued on in lonely lunar orbit in *Columbia*, Aldrin carefully piloted the *Eagle* down towards the surface of the moon.

Unable to see exactly what was beneath him, Aldrin flew beyond the chosen landing site in the Sea of Tranquillity. Fuel was low, and the surface now beneath them was strewn with large boulders. Urgently, he and Armstrong looked around for a smoother spot on which to come down. In the nick of time, they found one. Soon afterwards, Armstrong spoke the first words from the moon, *"Houston, Tranquillity Base here. The* Eagle *has landed."* Had they flown for just 40 seconds more, they would have run out of fuel and crashed.

Almost seven hours later, a TV camera on the outside of the *Eagle* showed Armstrong dressed in a moonsuit climbing gingerly down the module's steps towards the surface of the moon. A great moment had arrived, perhaps the greatest in all exploration: *"That's one small step for a man,"* crackled the radio, *"one giant leap for mankind."* At 3.56 a.m. (BST), on 21 July 1969, a human being was standing on the moon.

Shortly afterwards, Aldrin joined his commander. For two and a quarter hours the pair bounced about, collecting moon rocks, conducting scientific experiments and taking photographs. When their time was up, they returned to the *Eagle* and flew the top half of it, the Ascent Stage, back to Collins in the waiting Command Module. The remains of the *Eagle* were abandoned in space, and *Apollo* struck out on the long journey home.

One last peril remained: re-entering the earth's atmosphere. To save *Apollo 11* and its crew from being vaporized, the Command Module was fitted with a giant heat shield that glowed at 1,260°C on re-entry. Fortunately, it did its job. Once the danger was over, the astronauts slowed the module's descent by opening a series of parachutes.

Swaying gently, *Columbia* floated down, down, down until it splashed softly into the Pacific Ocean. Minutes later, rescue craft were on the scene, lifting the spacecraft and its crew to safety.

The final chapter in the great book of exploration had been written. Or had it? In the eyes of many scientists and explorers, far from being the last story in an old book, the Apollo 11 adventure was the first in a thrilling new one... ✪

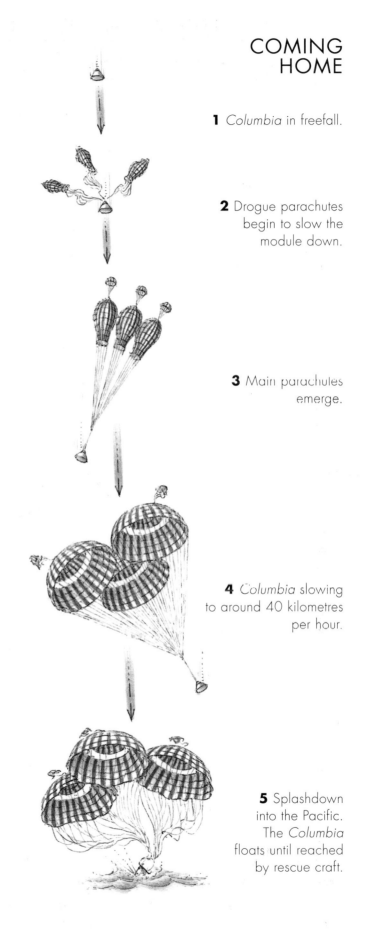

1 *Columbia* in freefall.

2 Drogue parachutes begin to slow the module down.

3 Main parachutes emerge.

4 *Columbia* slowing to around 40 kilometres per hour.

5 Splashdown into the Pacific. The *Columbia* floats until reached by rescue craft.

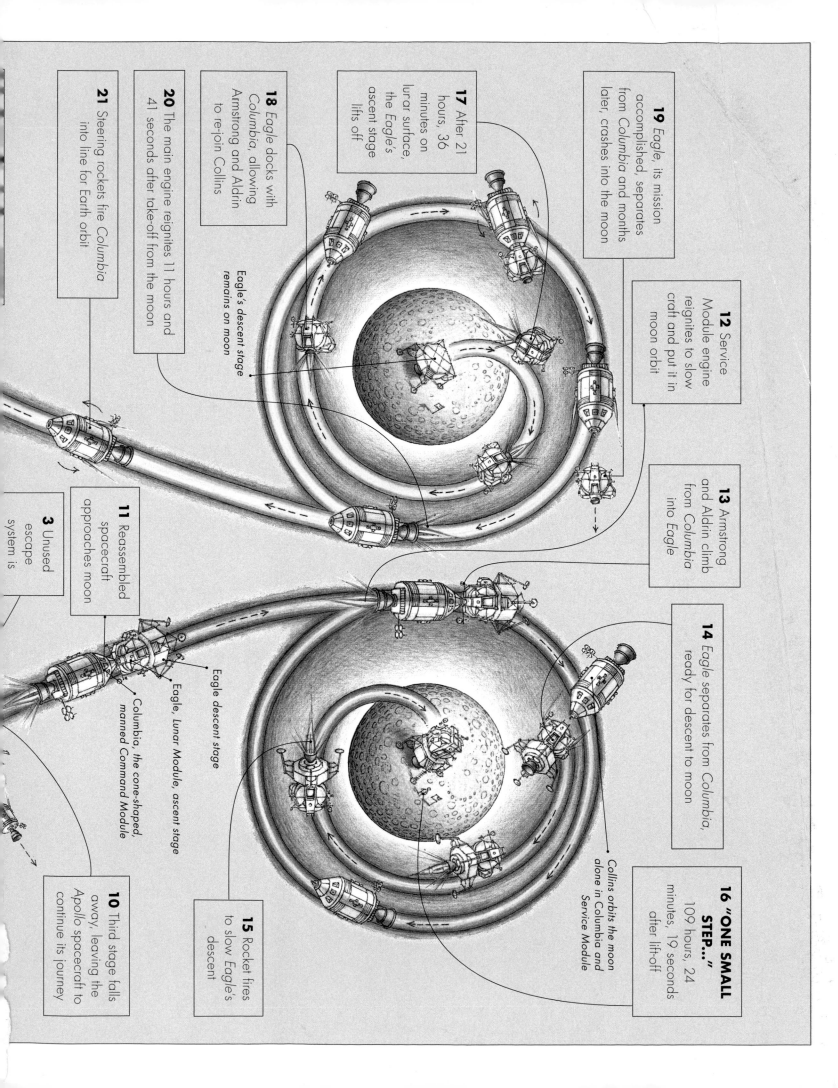

19 *Eagle*, its mission accomplished, separates from *Columbia* and months later, crashes into the moon

12 Service Module engine reignites to slow craft and put it in moon orbit

13 Armstrong and Aldin climb from *Columbia* into *Eagle*

17 After 21 hours, 36 minutes on lurar surface, the *Eagle*'s ascent stage lifts off

18 *Eagle* docks with *Columbia*, allowing Armstrong and Aldrin to rejoin Collins

20 The main engine reignites 11 hours and 41 seconds after take-off from the moon

21 Steering rockets fire *Columbia* into line for Earth orbit

Eagle's descent stage remains on moon

14 *Eagle* separates from *Columbia*, ready for descent to moon

Collins orbits the moon alone in Columbia and Service Module

16 "ONE SMALL STEP..."
109 hours, 24 minutes, 19 seconds after lift-off

11 Reassembled spacecraft approaches moon

3 Unused escape system is

Eagle, Lunar Module, ascent stage

Columbia, the cone-shaped, manned Command Module

Eagle descent stage

15 Rocket fires to slow *Eagle*'s descent

10 Third stage falls away, leaving the Apollo spacecraft to continue its journey

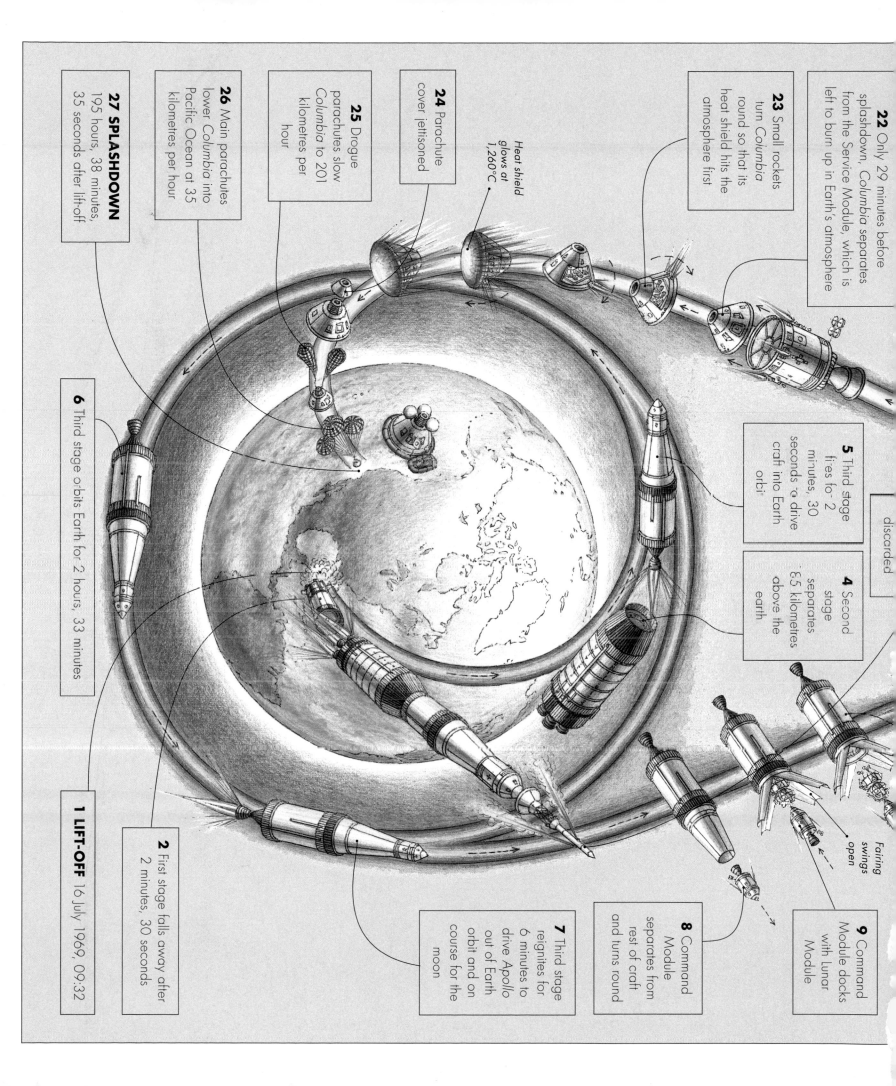

22 Only 29 minutes before splashdown, Columbia separates from the Service Module, which is left to burn up in Earth's atmosphere

23 Small rockets turn Columbia round so that its heat shield hits the atmosphere first

Heat shield glows at 1,260°C

24 Parachute cover jettisoned

25 Drogue parachutes slow Columbia to 201 kilometres per hour

26 Main parachutes lower Columbia into Pacific Ocean at 35 kilometres per hour

27 SPLASHDOWN 195 hours, 38 minutes, 35 seconds after lift-off

discarded

5 Third stage fires for 2 minutes, 30 seconds to drive craft into Earth orbit

4 Second stage separates 85 kilometres above the earth

6 Third stage orbits Earth for 2 hours, 33 minutes

1 LIFT-OFF 16 July 1969, 09:32

2 First stage falls away after 2 minutes, 30 seconds

7 Third stage reignites for 6 minutes to drive Apollo out of Earth orbit and on course for the moon

8 Command Module separates from rest of craft and turns round

Fairing swings open

9 Command Module docks with Lunar Module

INDEX

GLOSSARY

Some of the unusual words in this book are explained below. Words that appear in **bold** *have entries of their own.*

AMBASSADOR – an official who represents his or her country in a foreign land

AMBER – the fossilized sap of a coniferous (evergreen) tree

ASTROLOGER – someone who believes in the power of the moon, the sun, the planets and the stars to influence events and behaviour on Earth

BILGES – the lowest part of the interior of a ship's hull, where water from leaks builds up

BOTANIST – someone who studies plant life

BOW – the front of a ship

CARAVAN – several merchants and their **pack animals** travelling together

CARAVEL – a small but seaworthy European ship, developed in the late Middle Ages, with three masts and triangular sails

CAREEN – to turn a ship on its side on a sloping shore in order to repair or clean it

CARRACK – a large European cargo vessel, developed from the **caravel**, with three masts and, usually, square sails

CAULK – to fill the gaps between the planks of a ship's hull in order to make it watertight

CHART – a map of the sea, showing coastlines, depths and so on

CHRONOMETER – a clock that keeps accurate time when being moved about

COMPASS – a device for indicating north

CREVASSE – a deep crack in a surface of ice

DESTROYER – a small modern warship

DRAUGHT – the depth of water a ship needs to float

DRY DOCK – a dock drained of water so a ship can be built or repaired

EQUATOR – the imaginary line running round the middle of the earth

FLAGSHIP – the ship that carries the admiral of a fleet

FREIGHTER – a modern cargo-carrying ship

GEOLOGIST – someone who studies rocks and their formation

GLACIER – a slow-moving river of ice

GRAVITY – a force attracting one object to another. The heavier an object, the more powerful its gravity – so the sun's gravity is greater than the earth's, which is greater than the moon's

HANGAR – a large shed in which aircraft are housed

HATCH – a water- or air-tight doorway leading in or out of a ship or spaceship

HOLD – a space inside a ship for storing cargo and supplies

HOPPER – a large container for solid materials, such as sand or coal

HULL – the outer skin of a ship

INCANTATION – a religious chant

JUNK – a Chinese ship with square sails and a high **bow** and **stern**

KEEL – the backbone of a ship: a bar of wood or steel running the full length of the bottom of the **hull**

LATEEN – a triangular sail

LATITUDE – the distance north or south of the **equator**

LOGBOOK – a book in which a ship's progress is recorded

LONGITUDE – the distance east or west of a given point on the earth's surface

LOOM – a machine for weaving cloth from thread

MISSIONARY – a person who travels to another land in order to spread their religion

MODULE – a section or part

MONSOON – a tropical wet season, often featuring strong winds

MUTINY – a rebellion by soldiers or sailors who refuse to obey their officers

NATURALIST – a person who studies nature and the natural world

OASIS – a well or pool of fresh water in the desert

OBSERVATORY – a place for observing the sky with a telescope

PACK ANIMAL – an animal, such as a horse or donkey, used for carrying heavy loads on its back

PADDLE STEAMER – a steam-powered boat driven by revolving paddles on the sides or at the **stern**

PARCHMENT – tough paper made from animal skin

PHARAOH – an all-powerful ruler of ancient Egypt

PLANKTON – masses of tiny sea-dwelling creatures

PORT – a harbour; also the left side of a ship

PORTER – a person whose job is to carry loads

PORTHOLE – a round window in a ship or spaceship

PRESSURIZED – air-tight, so that the inside pressure does not vary

PROW – the **bow** (front) of a ship

RAM – a wooden or metal bar sticking out of the front of a ship for attacking enemy vessels

RAPIDS – places where a river runs swiftly over a shallow rocky bed

REEF – dangerous rocks on, or just beneath, the surface of the sea

RIGGING – the ropes and sails of a ship

RIVET – a metal fastener that, unlike a nail, sticks out from both sides of the objects being joined

RUDDER – a central steering board at the **stern** of a ship

SAGA – an ancient Scandinavian tale of daring deeds

SATELLITE – a man-made or natural object that circles (orbits) round a heavenly body, such as the earth

SCALE – to climb

SCURVY – a disease caused by lack of vitamin C

SEAMS – lines where the separate planks of a ship's **hull** meet. They are made watertight by **caulking**

SEISMIC – relating to movement beneath the surface of the earth or another heavenly body

SHERPA – a person from the Sola Khumbu district in Nepal, often employed on climbing expeditions

SHOAL – dangerous rocks, coral or sand just beneath the surface of the sea

STARBOARD – the right side of a ship

STERN – the back of a ship

STRAKE – a plank of wood used in shipbuilding

STRATOSPHERE – a high level of Earth's atmosphere where there is little oxygen

SUB-ATOMIC – smaller than a single atom

TACK – to sail into the wind by zigzagging

TERRAIN – landscape

TILLER – the steering pole attached to a ship's **rudder**

TRIBUTE – money or goods paid to a powerful ruler to gain or keep their favour

WINCH – a winding machine

WINDLASS – a machine for lowering or raising heavy objects into a ship's **hold**

SOURCES

Writers and illustrators owe a debt of gratitude to the authors and artists whose works inspire them. Stewart Ross and Stephen Biesty searched in lots and lots of books for details that would make the text and pictures of Into the Unknown *authentic. The following were some of the most useful:*

Aldrin, Buzz: **Magnificent Desolation: The Long Journey Home from the Moon**

Armstrong, Neil; Dick, Steven; Jacobs, Robert; Moore, Constance; Ulrich, Bertram: **America in Space: NASA's First Fifty Years**

Baker, Simon: **The Ship: Retracing Captain Cook's** *Endeavour* **Voyage**

Brown, Robin: **Marco Polo: The Incredible Journey**

Cohen, J. M. (translator): **The Four Voyages of Christopher Columbus: Being His Own Log-book, Letters and Dispatches**

Cook, James (selected and edited by Philip Edwards): **The Journals**

Cunliffe, Barry: **The Extraordinary Voyage of Pytheas the Greek**

Fleming, Fergus: **Tales of Endurance**

Frank, Katherine: **A Voyager Out: The Life of Mary Kingsley**

Hillary, Edmund: **High Adventure**

Horton, Edward: **The Age of the Airship**

Hunt, John: **The Ascent of Everest**

Jeal, Tim: **Livingstone**

Jones, Gwyn (editor): **Erik the Red and Other Icelandic Sagas**

Keay, John (editor): **The Royal Geographical Society History of World Exploration**

Kingsley, Mary: **Travels in West Africa**

Landstrom, Bjorn: **Columbus**

Landstrom, Bjorn: **The Quest for India**

Latham, R. E. (translator): **The Travels of Marco Polo**

Levathes, Louise: **When China Ruled the Seas**

Livingstone, David and Charles: **Expedition to the Zambesi**

Malkus, Alida: **Exploring the Sky and Sea: Auguste and Jacques Piccard**

Roseman, Christina Horst: **Pytheas of Massalia:** *On the Ocean*: **Text, Translation and Commentary**

Pigafetta, Antonio (translated by R. A. Skelton): **Magellan's Voyage: A Narrative Account of the First Circumnavigation**

Severin, Tim: **The Brendan Voyage**

Venables, Stephen: **Everest: Summit of Achievement**

ACKNOWLEDGEMENTS

The editors and publisher gratefully acknowledge permission for the use of the following material:

Chapter 1 Excerpts from **Pytheas of Massalia:** *On the Ocean*: **Text, Translation and Commentary** by Christina Horst Roseman, published by Ares Publishers, Inc., 1994.

Chapter 3 Excerpt from page 31 of **When China Ruled the Seas** by Louise Levathes, published by Oxford University Press, 1996.

Chapter 5 Excerpts from **Magellan's Voyage: A Narrative Account of the First Circumnavigation** by Antonio Pigafetta (translated by R. A. Skelton), published by Yale University Press, 1969.

Every reasonable effort has been made to trace ownership of and/or secure permission for the use of copyrighted material. If notified of any omission, the editors and publisher will gladly make any necessary corrections in future printings.

If you enjoyed this book, you might also enjoy:

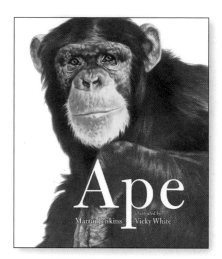

Ape
ISBN 978-1-4063-1929-3

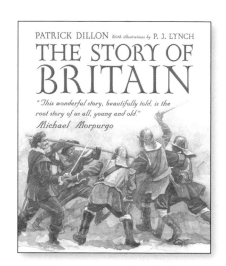

The Story of Britain
ISBN 978-1-4063-4860-6

Can We Save the Tiger?
ISBN 978-1-4063-3208-7

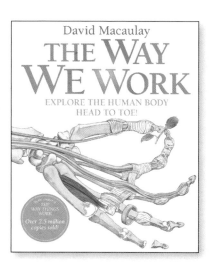

The Way We Work
ISBN 978-1-4063-2222-4

Available from all good booksellers

www.walker.co.uk